The World Wars

THE FIRST
WORLD WAR

Edited by Stewart Ross
from an original text by
Annie Brown, Lionel Dumarche, Philippe Glorennec
Jean-Marcel Humbert and Jean-Pierre Verney
English translation by
Paul Foulkes

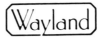

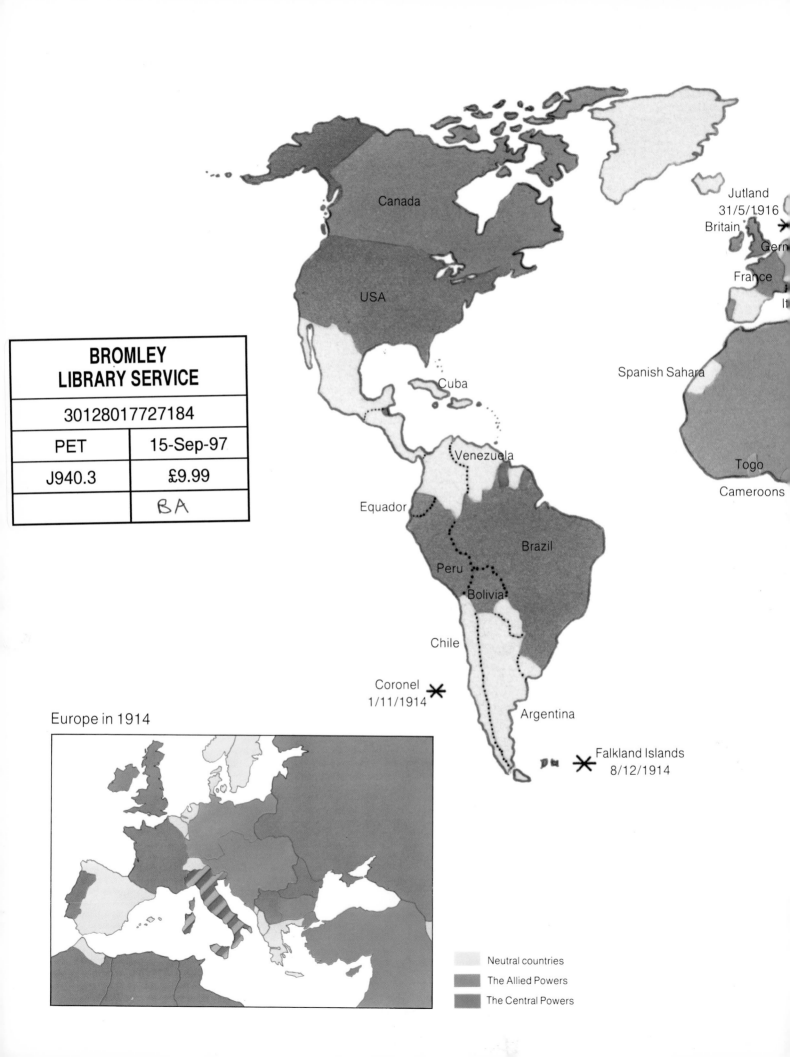

Canada

USA

Cuba

Venezuela

Equador

Peru

Bolivia

Brazil

Chile

Coronel
1/11/1914

Argentina

Falkland Islands
8/12/1914

Jutland
31/5/1916

Britain

Germ

France

It

Spanish Sahara

Togo

Cameroons

Europe in 1914

	Neutral countries
	The Allied Powers
	The Central Powers

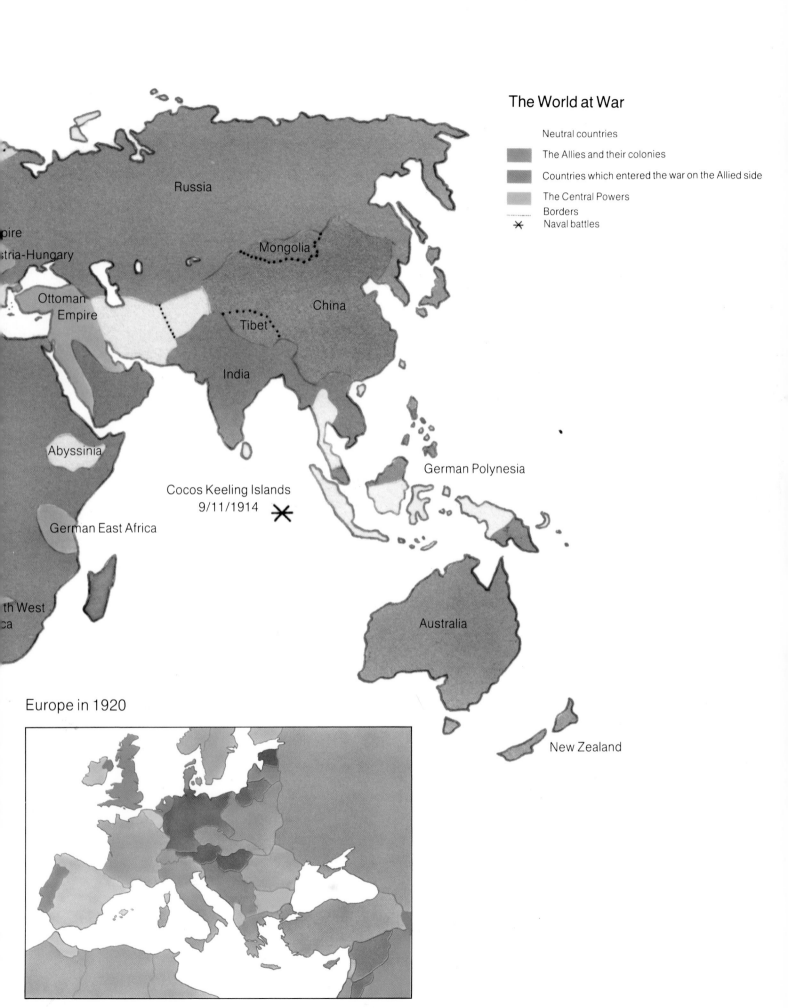

The World at War

Neutral countries
The Allies and their colonies
Countries which entered the war on the Allied side
The Central Powers
Borders
✳ Naval battles

Russia

Mongolia

China

Ottoman Empire

Tibet

India

Abyssinia

Cocos Keeling Islands
9/11/1914 ✳

German Polynesia

German East Africa

th West
ca

Australia

Europe in 1920

New Zealand

pire
stria-Hungary

© 1986 Casterman, originally published in French under the title *Les Jours de l'Histoire: 14–18 La Première Guerre Mondiale*.

© This edition Wayland (Publishers) Ltd
Published pursuant to an agreement
with Casterman, Paris

First published in the UK in 1989 by
Wayland (Publishers) Ltd
61 Western Road
Hove, East Sussex BN3 1DU

British Library Cataloguing in Publication Data
Ross, Stewart
    The First World War.
    1. World War 1
    940.3

ISBN 1 85210 796 0

Picture Credits
ECPA: back cover, 9t, 61b/JL Charmet Collection: 10t, 11t/R Dazy Collection: 10b, 42b/Documentation Française: front cover/Imperial War Museum, London: 11b, 13t, 31/Musée de l'Armée, Paris: 8b, 9b, 10b, 11t, 12, 15, 22b, 29bl, 35b, 69/ Musée de l'Armée, Brussels: 13b/BDIC – Musée d'Histoire, University of Paris: 20b, 47t, 59t/Coll. part DR: 20t, 62, 68/Tallandier Collection: 26t&b, 46, 47b, 48t, 49t/Roger-Viollet: 30b, 33b, 38, 43b, 44b, 45t, 51t, 55b/M Toulet Collection: 34b/ Credit Line: USA: 45b, 57bl/Photothèque SNCF: 64t. All other archive documents reproduced by Marcel Moulin, © Association pour un Musée Vivant de la Guerre 1914–18.

Contents

Foreword

A list of names carved on a war memorial, in honour of the dead; each year on 11 November, the anniversary of Armistice Day. Photos of trenches in which corpses lie half buried in the mud. The memories of a grandmother whose father was killed on the Somme, or at Verdun . . . Powerful as these images are, the war of 1914–18 was much more than a set of pictures from the past. When it began, it was like all the wars of the nineteenth century, with its brightly coloured uniforms and cavalry charges. However, after only a few months everything changed. It turned into a war of attrition; the importance of the individual was replaced by that of objects, machines, technology and economics. Until then, all wars had only involved a small number of countries. The one that broke out in 1914 spread quickly to engulf the whole world. In Europe, the Middle East, Asia and Africa, people fought on land, at sea and in the air. Within the four years that the conflict lasted, the world changed: the United States became aware of its power, while that of the Old World declined. Some countries disappeared from the map altogether, such as Montenegro and Austria-Hungary, while others, like Russia, changed greatly or were re-born, like Poland, and some, like Yugoslavia and Czechoslovakia, were created out of old empires.

Naturally, not everyone's experience of the war was the same. This story of great upheavals concerns not only the small group of men who decided and directed the events. The vast majority of those involved were people caught up in something over which they had no control. The Orbec family, for example, had a small farm at Quatre-Mare, near Louviers in Normandy. In August 1914, the father left, called up at Rouen to the 239th infantry regiment. His wife had to bring in the harvest helped only by her children. Weeks and months went by. In his letters from the trenches, the father asked for news of his farm and gave

advice on what to do. He said little about the war; the welfare of his animals and his crops meant far more to him than military operations and political manoeuvres. Through his wife's replies he received news, and learned of family bereavements: 'Yesterday the police came from Louviers to tell Félicie that Jules was killed in Artois. Your two brothers are dead; you alone are left. I pray hard that this horrible war will not take you as well . . .' From 1915, on very occasional leave, the two were reunited, and the father was able to hug his wife and children again. But after a few days, he had to tear himself away and go back to the front. His wife remained alone, in mortal fear of a visit from the mayor or the police carrying the terrible news. Whatever the newspapers may have said about the world's fate being decided at Verdun, the Chemin des Dames, or wherever, what mattered to her was the life of just one man.

The armistice was the only time when she read a paper from beginning to end,

and even then she waited for a letter from her husband before she really believed it. When eventually he did come back, demobilized in 1919, she hoped that life would return to pre-war days, when after supper he used to smoke his pipe in the corner by the stove. However, he now spoke even less than before, and never about what he had gone through. She respected his silence. In France, and all over Europe, so many had left never to return. The war had shattered the world, destroyed empires, and caused dreadful slaughter, but it had spared her husband.

A division of Zouaves, *French shock troops, going into the attack*

Before the tragedy: on 28 June 1914, Franz Ferdinand and Princess Sophia leave the town hall of Sarajevo, saluted by the authorities. A few minutes later they fell to the bullets of a Serbian terrorist.

A French mobilization notice of 2 August 1914

The First Casualties

Since the end of the nineteenth century, tension in Europe had been mounting. By 1906, the French and Germans were at loggerheads. In the Balkans, Russia and Austria-Hungary watched small states quarrelling over the spoils of the decaying Ottoman Empire. Among the governments of Europe, there were those that felt 'a nice little war' would settle these problems once and for all.

Threatening alliances

After a humiliating defeat by the Prussians in 1870–71, France had lost the provinces of Alsace and Lorraine to the new German Empire. The loss continued to rankle with the French, and in 1894 they acquired a powerful ally in the East, Russia and its enormous army. Britain, meanwhile, was worried by Germany's growing economic strength, and watched Kaiser Wilhelm II, with a distrustful eye as he strengthened his navy. 'Our future lies at sea,' he had said. The British government leaned towards France and signed the *Entente Cordiale* in 1904. The French general staff saw this as a guarantee of victory in their claim for the lost provinces, for France now had as an ally the foremost naval power in the world. However, as it was the strongest power in central Europe, Germany was not afraid of war. Joined with Austria-Hungary and Italy by the Triple Alliance, its army was unequalled. If the French wanted revenge, let them try.

The death of an archduke

By 1913, some of the German military commanders were waiting for an excuse for war. It came the next year. On 28 June 1914, the Austrian Crown Prince, Archduke Franz Ferdinand, and his wife visited Sarajevo, capital of Bosnia-Herzegovina, a small state annexed by Austria-Hungary not long before. The carriage of the heir to the Hapsburg throne took a wrong turning on its route through the city. As it stopped, a young man rushed forward and fired twice. The Archduke and his wife collapsed and died. An Austrian enquiry quickly established that the young killer, Princip, belonged to a Serbian terrorist organization and had come straight from a meeting of an anti-Austrian society in Belgrade, the Serbian capital. On 23 July, Austria sent Serbia a list of demands, knowing that acceptance was impossible. In fact, Serbia agreed to most of them, but Austria would not be swayed from its purpose. On 28 July 1914, Austria declared war on Serbia. At once Russia began to mobilize its army to help Serbia. From then on the alliances took their course. On 31 July Austria-Hungary mobilized, and France followed suit. Germany declared war on Russia on 1 August, and then on France on 3 August. The same day, the Germans invaded neutral Belgium and Luxembourg, hoping to outflank the French. On 4 August, Britain pledged to help Belgium and declared war on Germany. Within a few days, the whole of Europe was ablaze, and everyone was blaming everyone else for having started the fire. In fact, everyone was to blame: Austria for starting war with Serbia, Russia for being the first to mobilize, Germany for urging her Austrian ally to be unyielding, France for failing to solve the crisis, and Britain for standing aloof, allowing the Germans to believe she would never defend Belgium. Whatever the reasons, the terrible engine of war had been set in motion. Nothing could stop it now.

Above: A French cuirassier in 1914. The French army, like others in Europe, still had many cavalry units, some of which were armed as they had been in the Napoleanic wars of 1799 to 1815.

A German propaganda postcard dating from early in the war. On the left-hand side of the balance, an Austrian and a Prussian with his spiked helmet make the bar tilt towards their side, owing to the weight of the shell, which represents their powerful armaments. On the right are a Frenchman with the face of Napolean III, a little Belgian, a beared Russian, and an Englishman smoking his pipe. A Japanese (Britain's ally since 1902), and a Montenegran are clinging to their feet. A Serb, blamed for starting the whole thing, is sitting above them. On the plinth a Turk, an American and an Italian, as yet neutral, are waiting before committing themselves.

DEUTSCHLAND IM EUROPÄISCHEN „GLEICHGEWICHT"

Gone for a Summer

A French infantryman of 1914, with his blue coat and scarlet trousers. French generals regarded their infantry as the best soldiers in the world. Supported by 75mm field guns and armed with their Lebel rifles, they were bound to bring victory.

Paris, Gare de l'Est, 2 August 1914: a train-load of reservists is about to leave for garrisons in eastern France. On the platform, women are crying. The men at the windows of compartments are waving their caps. Some are joking: 'We'll cut the Emperor's moustache!' 'The train will not stop this side of the Rhine!' On the carriage doors there are chalk graffiti: 'Pleasure trip to Berlin', 'Non-stop to Germany'. However, the atmosphere is more serious. They are leaving to do their duty, no more. Reconquest of Alsace-Lorraine? Only journalists talk about that. If mobilization has caused a flutter of anxiety in the countryside (for the men will not be there for the harvest), the dominant feeling everywhere is that of a nation justified in defending itself.

At stations in Berlin the same scenes are repeated. Only the wording on the doors of the carriages is different: 'Nach Paris' (To Paris), 'Cheap seats for France'. There are the same farewell embraces and tearful eyes watching the men go away. Civilians and soldiers are convinced that Germany is fully in the right: 'We had to challenge the powers that are trying to encircle and crush us!'

In both countries, mobilization passed without incident. The authorities had feared acts of disobedience; in France, for example, they had compiled lists of suspects, socialists, pacifists and anarchists who might have resisted the call-up. However, these lists remained unused. There were very few deserters. The police were given the job of examining the health of those who claimed to be unfit: anyone who attempted to avoid having to do his duty was quickly returned to his unit.

War plans

On both sides people agreed that the war would be short. 'Back for Christmas', they said at the Gare de l'Est. Their

opposite numbers in Berlin echoed the same sentiments; the cafés of Alexander Platz were full of instant experts: '. . . Two months at the most . . . No industrial country can allow its economy to be disrupted by a long war!'

The campaign plans of the two sides were, in fact, based on just this assumption. For von Moltke, the German Commander-in-Chief, the offensive was to be a lightning blow: 'In two weeks our right wing of 800,000 men will sweep all before it. With Belgium and France invaded, Paris must surrender . . . England will not even have time to intervene!'

General Joffre, the French Commander-in-Chief since 1911, knew the plan but regarded it as illusory. 'Germany will have to fight in the East as well, to stop the Russian "steamroller". But it lacks the men to wage war on two fronts. The Belgians will hold out and we shall help them if need be. Then as soon as they are mobilized, our infantry will attack in Lorraine.' The general staffs on both sides liked to dream of offensives, of putting into practice the manoeuvres they had rehearsed so often on the blackboards of their military academies.

A German infantryman of 1914 in his grey-green uniform. The German army was led by an excellent officer corps. They also had greater fire-power — more machine-guns and heavy guns — than the French.

In Paris and Berlin, reservists get ready to leave.

Invasion

Early on 2 August, notices throughout France announced a general mobilization. At Jonchery, a small village in eastern France, there was chaos. 'We are just a couple of steps from the German border!' Everyone was hurriedly getting ready to leave – the men to their units, the women, children and old people to escape an expected German attack. In this atmosphere, rumours thrived: 'The Prussians are coming!' Somebody had seen them, or thought they had.

A corporal dies

When corporal Peugeot and his patrol heard the cry, 'The Prussians!', he thought it was yet another false alarm. But the German bullet which killed him moments later was real enough. He was the first French casualty in a war as yet unnamed. The next day, Germany declared war on France and invaded Belgium. There, near Dinant, Jules Ponchard was waiting with his comrades of the 33rd infantry regiment. He had marched, stopped, and marched again under a blazing sun, getting more and more tired and disheartened. He joked to calm his nerves: 'Where are those Prussians? Let's send them home!'

The attack came soon enough. The lieutenant drew his sword for the charge. Ahead of them a German machine-gun poured out its deadly fire, littering the field with mutilated bodies. Ponchard was unharmed, but all around him his friends lay dead or writhing in agony. Jules remembered his jokes and looked again at the serious truth around him: he saw that bullets killed.

The French general staff had called for a 'fresh and merry' war, involving merciless offensives. Thousands of useless deaths resulted, but the Germans, more numerous and with the immense fire power of their heavy artillery, were not pushed back. The Ponchard family thought of their son who had missed the harvest, but were sure he would return soon. The newspapers were full of nothing but great victories: the French have taken Mulhouse . . . Alsace will become French again . . . all will soon be back to normal!

Paris threatened

The facts, however, were very different. Mulhouse had to be abandoned a day after being taken. The Germans swallowed Belgium in one gulp, and thousands of refugees swarmed towards France. By 28 August, the French government could no longer conceal the truth; the Germans were at the River Somme, and not, as they had claimed, still in Belgium. Panic broke out, exacerbated by the arrival of refugees from the battle front. France had been invaded. Its armies were forced to retreat from the River Oise to the Meuse, unable to resist the German advance. The mood in France had shifted from calm certainty to deep anxiety.

On the evening of 2 September a special train, with all its lights dimmed,

On the roads of Belgium and northern France, the chaos was incredible. Civilians piled their belongings on carts and fled from the threatened regions, often becoming mixed up with retreating soldiers. Not only did they impede troop movements, but also spread anxiety among those people who stayed behind.

Above: *German infantry in spiked helmets crossing the flowering fields of Brabant in August 1914. The Belgians, first to be attacked, were overwhelmed by the much larger German forces. Nevertheless, the concrete forts of Liège and Namur held up the German advance for six days, finally falling on 13 August.*

Right: *August 1914. Two wounded Belgian soldiers limp from the battlefield. After fierce fighting at Mons and Charleroi, the French and British were unable to hold the German advance. Belgian troops regrouped around the fort at Antwerp, while the French retreated on 25 August.*

left Paris taking the government to Bordeaux. Joffre, the French Commander-in-Chief, had stated that he could not defend the city against the Germans, and the government could not continue under direct threat from the enemy. By 3 September, the Germans were holding Château-Thierry and Creil, a mere 29 kilometres (18 miles) from Paris. Against the clear sky they could see the Eiffel Tower. Their planes flew over the capital, showering the bewildered citizens with propaganda leaflets. 'Parisians, surrender! Our armies have entered your city!'

The French did not know what to do. Should they declare Paris an open city, and give it up without a fight to the Germans, whom French propaganda had constantly portrayed as beasts who would not respect its people or monuments? Should they hold out, and prepare for a seige, as they had done in 1870, that 'terrible year' which older Parisians still remembered, when almost two million people had been shut up within the walls? Many people preferred to flee, setting off in carts carrying their most valued possessions. Almost no one believed that Paris could be saved.

13

Britain to the Rescue

The defence of Paris was entrusted to the 65-year-old General Gallieni. It seemed an almost impossible task. On 27 August, the city had only 43 days' worth of bread, and enough meat to last just 12 days. During the past three weeks, housewives had emptied the grocery shops. A few herds of cattle and sheep, had hastily been brought in to graze on the lawns of the Bois de Boulogne. Gallieni, however, was determined to hold out. On 3 September, the Germans, having taken Chantilly, started a strange manoeuvre. Instead of moving directly on Paris, they deviated towards Meaux. Von Moltke's plan was to by-pass the city to the east and south, and spring a trap on the whole allied army, forcing it to surrender within a week.

The fate of France

Joffre had to decide whether to retreat and try to regroup on the Seine, or to exploit the situation and attack on the River Marne. Urged on by Gallieni, Joffre quickly chose to attack. However, his troops were exhausted after two weeks of retreat, and 200,000 men had already been lost. A great deal now depended on the small but highly trained British Expeditionary Force, which had moved rapidly to France on the outbreak of hositilities. But first their commander, Marshal French, had to be won over. 'England's honour is at stake, sir!', urged Joffre. 'I'll do my best,' French replied. 'What did he say?', asked Joffre, who spoke no English. 'He said yes,' the interpreter replied.

The orders for 5 September were crucial: 'Men, we are on the verge of a battle that will decide this country's fate. We urge you not to look back . . . Any unit unable to advance must at all costs hold the ground it has won and, if necessary, die where it is rather than retreat . . .' At dawn, the divisions brought in by rail and by forced marches were ready for action. On the roads to the front, police and cavalry were stationed, with orders to stop deserters and send them back to fight, or to face a court martial and possibly execution.

Paris saved

The attack began on 5 September. The French under General Manoury hurled themselves at the German right. Officers, with sabres drawn, led the charge. However, the attackers were cut down by well-entrenched German machine-guns. By the next day, the battle had spread along a front from Senlis to Verdun. Nearly two million men were involved. The German guns boomed ceaselessly, while in the villages fierce hand-to-hand fighting often ended in bayonet scuffles. Joffre threw in all his troops, for he had no alternative but to attack. In the end his plan paid off. Between 7 and 9 September, although the French made no decisive gains, the British forced the Germans to retreat 20 kilometres (12 miles), and recaptured la Ferté-sous-Jouarre. To avoid being surrounded, the German first army under von Kluck, which had threatened Paris a week earlier, began to fall back. Then, on 10 September, the Germans gave the order for a general retreat. The French, exhausted and with enough

ammunition for only three more days, were unable to pursue the enemy. The Germans crossed the Marne and retired to the River Aisne. Von Moltke's plan had failed, and Paris was saved. But it was now clear that the war would last longer than everyone had dreamed.

An incident in the battle of the Marne: the taking of Barcy on 6 September 1914, painted by an unknown artist.

An artillery captain killed at the Marne, in September 1914. Many artists and writers died at the front. One of them was Lieutenant Péguy, killed on 5 September 1914. Earlier he had written this poem, foretelling his own death:

How fortunate are those who enter the warm earth
Killed in a just war;
How fortunate to die for a little land,
To find a noble death . . .
How fortunate are those who die for a hearthside
And the little treasures of home.

War on Several Fronts

A Cossack charge on the Russian front in 1914. Disorganized and badly equipped, the Tsar's army relied on its cavalry to sweep into Germany and Austria.

Confident in the power of her huge armies, Russia attacked Germany on 12 August 1914, without waiting for complete mobilization. Brushing aside some weak German forces, the Russian army invaded part of East Prussia. The Germans were furious, and fearful that the dreaded Cossacks might set foot on Prussian soil. Horrifying stories were told about these irregular troops from southern Russia: they buried their prisoners alive, cut off their heads, burned whole villages and crops, and raped women. 'Our children will be massacred by these wild hordes! Where is the army?' the Berlin press demanded angrily.

Meanwhile the Allies rejoiced: 'The Russian steamroller is moving!' 'The Cossacks are five days from Berlin', read the French headlines. But things were not as rosy as they appeared. The Russian army lacked discipline, competent generals and, above all, weapons and ammunition.

Defeat

The German general staff reacted swiftly to the Russian threat. On 23 August, Hindenburg and Ludendorff, who had recently been appointed to command the eastern front, decided to concentrate the bulk of their troops against one of the two Russian armies which were ranged against them.

This involved few risks, as the Russian telegraph messages were not being sent in code, and so the Germans knew the invaders' plans. Attacking on 26 August, the Germans took the Russians by surprise. Hampered by bad roads and lack of food, the Russians were crushed in three days at Tannenberg. Over 100,000 prisoners were captured. The other Russian army was soon pushed back over the border.

Along the whole eastern front, the Russians and the Germans remained locked in a bloody struggle, while for months Austria-Hungary tried vainly to crush Serbia.

King Peter holds out

Certain of their numerical superiority and crushing fire power, since early August the over-confident Austrian officers had regarded the offensive against the Serbs as a simple matter. 'These pig breeders will be brought to heel in three days!' The Austrian general staff was so confident of victory that the troops sent to crush Serbia had already been allocated a place on the front against Russia, in Galicia. However, they were up against a small determined force, fired with the courage and pride of a people defending their homeland. In one week's fighting, the Austrians lost 23,000 men without taking an inch of ground. In December, with a fresh offensive threatening the Serbian capital, Belgrade, the old King Peter counter-attacked at the head of his troops. He won a resounding victory. Allied propaganda showed him attacking the enemy, armed with nothing more than a rifle and forty cartridges. On 15 December, Serbia published a triumphant message: 'Not one armed enemy remains on our soil.'

On all sides plans for offensives had gone awry, as the generals had under-estimated the strength of the enemies they faced. By the end of 1914, it was clear that no army had the power to win the total victory which over-optimistic politicians had promised their people. On the eastern front and in France, exhausted armies dug themselves into deep trenches, going practically underground in order to stem the huge losses they had suffered during the first four months of fighting.

German cavalry and infantry reoccupying the burning town of Schaulen, East Prussia, in 1914.

Russian prisoners after the defeat at Tannenberg. Guarded by a German soldier, they are dragging their machine-guns.

Trench Warfare

For five days in September 1914, the French 18th infantry regiment pursued the German second army near Craonne on the Aisne. The Germans had retreated as fast as they had attacked, but then their undamaged artillery was moved back to check the French advance. Under the constant pounding of the German guns, the French had been forced to dig themselves in and hide. Almost overnight the fighting changed. From being a war of movement, it had now ground to a halt and become bogged down in trench warfare.

Hiding to survive

By December 1914, from the North Sea to the Swiss border, the front line consisted of two opposing fortified networks. The Germans were the first to build large, shored-up trenches for their infantry which had been pulled back after the battle of the Marne. In some places, the Germans used concrete to

reinforce their trenches. The French and British had to improvise and dig in where they were under enemy fire. Their infantry became navvies. In the front line they dug trenches about a metre (3½ feet) wide and over 2 metres (7 feet) deep, protected in places by armour plate and sometimes covered by flimsy roofs of branches and wire from fields nearby.

Under these conditions there could be no such thing as a surprise attack. If the enemy snipers saw a head pop up above the line of a trench, or the glow of a cigarette, they let loose with a hail of bullets. The artillery, placed some miles behind the lines, was now a crucial element in any attack. Heavy bombardments turned the front into a lunar landscape of hills and craters. If the shells fell short, a battery might wipe out men of its own side. Not until 1916 were all soldiers issued with steel helmets to protect them from head injuries. During an attack, every man gambled with his life. At the appointed time the men, often numbed and emboldened by alcohol, had to clamber out of their trenches and rush forward, under machine-gun fire and with shells exploding all around them, in the unbreathable atmosphere of poisonous gas and amid the blazing fury of the flame-throwers.

The infantrymen

Even when things were quiet, at the front, life was hardly bearable. Wading through the mire at the bottom of the trenches, unable to wash or shave, the flea-bitten soldiers were crowded into rat-infested underground shelters or dug-outs. Mail was brought from the rear. Soup, prepared in the second line, was carried forward by cooks who, bent double, came up the zig-zag connecting trenches. They risked their lives each day to bring food to those at the front.

But it was often cold and uneatable.

Periods of inactivity were spent playing cards or joking with friends. With the help of pitchers of cheap wine, they laughed at their lives which were barely liveable. Those who were skilled with their hands carved shell cases into ornaments and curios to adorn fireplaces after the war; others invented and made fearful weapons, cutting bullets to make 'dum-dums' which caused terrible injuries on impact.

Fraternization

Sometimes men sent to bring back water might meet enemy soldiers on the edge of a pond formed in a shell hole. Usually such encounters ended in a knife or bayonet fight, but sometimes the soldiers fraternized. 'After all, the lads over there are just poor blighters like us!' 'At Christmas, we even heard them singing!', a French soldier told his NCO. 'Perhaps, but we'll talk about it when they have gone home!', came the reply.

Summer 1918. German infantry leaving the front line to attack. In 1916 the distinctive spiked helmet had been replaced by a steel helmet which wrapped around the head for better protection.

19

A British naval gun-boring plant in 1916

War and Industry

A German notice reads: 'The best savings bank: war loans!'

After some weeks of fighting, commanders on both sides realized that the war would be a long one. Arms and ammunition were being used up at an unprecedented rate, and it became increasingly clear that the war would be won at home as much as at the front.

The provisions of war

In order to supply their armies and navies, the countries involved in the war became like gigantic factories, turning out countless numbers of guns, shells and uniforms. From 1915, France and Germany each produced 40 million rifle bullets and over 100,000 shells a day!

From large plants to tiny workshops, the whole of industry was geared to the war effort. Saucepan-makers turned out shell-cases; celluloid doll manufacturers converted to the production of gunpowder. Tens of thousands of women, and children under 18, were employed to replace the men who had been called up. In Germany and France, the army had to send back over 500,000 technicians and skilled workers from the front to operate machines or work at drawing-boards – work which was regarded as a top national priority. France used many foreign labourers, especially from its colonies. They were sent to work in factories and on the land.

In Marseilles alone, 120,000 Italians, 50,000 Indo-Chinese, 14,000 Spaniards, and 5,000 Madagascans worked in the factories and helped to build a new port. In Britain, which did not resort to conscription until 1916 and which was able to draw on its vast empire, the situation was never quite so desperate.

Germany was severely hampered by an Allied naval blockade, and became the first country to have to ration raw materials. She also rigorously exploited the countries she had conquered forcing local people to help in her war effort, and requisitioning food, vehicles and animals. In the end, the Germans resorted to rounding up large numbers of young workers and sending them to Germany where, together with prisoners of war, they were forced to replace the workers, miners and farmers who had gone off to the front.

State ownership

Turning a country's entire economy over to the war effort required planning and control on a massive scale. The state was now the main customer of all agricultural and industrial products, and could no longer afford to allow owners to organize their own production. Therefore, governments distributed both raw materials and labour, giving precise instructions regarding what to make, in what quantities and to what standards. All means of transport were liable to be requisitioned to move men, animals, arms and ammunition to the front. In Britain, factories were required by law to increase their output. Those that failed to do so received no more orders, and the work went to others which seemed more efficient. Competition was restricted; in many countries prices were fixed, and so was pay. This discipline was on the whole accepted by the trade unions, and there were very few strikes before 1916.

Astute industrialists and inventors were able to take advantage of state loans to build workshops and factories, where arms, planes, lorries and tanks were made on production lines after 1917. Unscrupulous dealers made large profits from war orders, for the authorities were often lax regarding working conditions and the quality of output. Some amassed huge fortunes, which they flaunted in showy luxury. For ordinary people – hit by price rises, rationing and the absence of all their young men – that was especially unbearable.

Below: In all countries, the state provided the finance for the war. Lacking ready cash to pay suppliers, governments needed to borrow from their citizens. These French savers are shown at a bank counter, depositing their savings.

Bottom picture: European armies were swelled by recruits from colonies around the world.

Propaganda

A huge volume of mail passed daily between home and the front. After all, what could be more natural than the civilians showing their support for the soldiers by sending them postcards. With grim sentimentality, their hackneyed themes — children, the flag, the Allies and the 'Boche' — sought to maintain the patriotic fervour.

Christmas 1914. Even before the naval blockade of Germany, English soldiers playfully imagine that a few slices of bread are enough to disarm starving Germans.

In 1915, some French papers claimed that the Germans' shells were made of cardboard, and that their shrapnel merely caused bruises. Meanwhile, German journalists wrote that 'French corpses smell worse than German ones'!

All the countries at war used propaganda, not so much to deceive as to keep up people's morale and fighting spirit. Here are some of the most frequently repeated claims. In 1915, the *Écho de Paris* stated that 'they [the Germans] cut the feet off the wounded and smash their skulls with rifle butts'. In 1914, the *Revue Hebdomadaire* told its readers: 'German officers are brutes; the only way they get their men to fight is at pistol point. Ours are brothers, big brothers, leading by gentle example!' Even German women's fashion was ridiculed; one sketch was captioned: 'A town gown adorned with sausage slices. Round the neck, a pretty chain of Frankfurters. Charming hat garnished with sauerkraut and pin in shape of fork!' The Germans lampooned the American President Wilson. Kaiser Wilhelm II called France a 'female country'.

The appearance of black soldiers at the front unleashed even more anti-French propaganda: 'The so-called democracies are mere hypocrites, sending barely civilized people to war!' They were called 'Jumbos', or 'woman-eaters'. In a cartoon, Senegalese children are promised: 'Be good and daddy will bring back a juicy steak of Germans!'

All this nonsense was spread not only by newspapers, posters, drawings, photographs and shows, but also on many objects such as cigarette packets, the covers of children's books, lamps, toys and much more. Advertisers made use of the situation. Because everyone was totally preoccupied with the war, it was used to help sell almost anything. For example, French advertisements for the purgative *Jubol* claimed that it 'dislodges microbes from the gut as swiftly as a *poilu* removes Germans from a trench'. A German tonic claimed to help soldiers to survive in the damp conditions of the trenches.

Governments found it easy to influence public opinion through total control of the Press. Censorship was established at the start of the war in all the countries involved. Any news that might harm national defence or morale – military information, criticisms of the government, or discouraging reports – was banned. From the outbreak of war, it was forbidden to publish lists of the dead and wounded in France. Instead, 'official' facts and figures were given, often quite different from the sad reality. In March 1916, the French *Petit Journal* stated that 'some of the soldiers accommodation at Verdun is fairly comfortable, with central heating and electricity.' The men at the front knew otherwise, as a letter from one of them made clear in November 1914: '. . . the sham cheerfulness attributed to the men, the pointedly colourful accounts of how the trenches are fitted out and the like; all this is just the invention of the press. We find it intolerable. The men are calm and resigned to the harsh realities of war, but they suffer from the cold and bad weather in dreadful misery . . .'

In all the countries at war, deliberate falsification of the facts caused a rift between the home front and the war front. On one side were those at home, surrounded by false news and distorted visions of the war; on the other side were those who were fighting in the front line, wanting no pity but angry that their suffering and sacrifices were being misrepresented and misunderstood. With conscious irony, they began to refer to themselves as the 'poor blighters up front'.

November 1914. This picture, used by German newspapers and also in those of neutral countries, shows 'decent German soldiers' sharing their bread and soup with children and refugees in the occupied territories.

The War of Photos

When used cleverly, photography could be a valuable propaganda weapon. On the left, German officers are shown receiving cups for winning a riding event in 1913. On the right is the same photo, which was given to the press by the Russians, with a caption about Germans brutally plundering the country houses of Russian aristocrats.

Battle for the Skies

An observation balloon (or 'sausage') slowly rising into the air, held by a cable. Sitting freezing in his basket, the observer could see a large area of enemy territory. The weak hulls of these balloons, filled with inflammable gas, made them liable to explode in flames if hit by bullets from an enemy plane.

In October 1914, two planes were jousting in the sky; one French, one German. The former's machine-gun rattled but then jammed. The mechanic stood up to try to fix it, but it didn't matter, for the German plane tipped over, crashed into the ground and instantly burst into flames. Thus ended the first ever aerial combat. Aeroplanes had become weapons of war alongside infantry and artillery. Yet at the outbreak of hostilities, few officers took them seriously. They were suitable for sport perhaps, but not for the army. The early machines were indeed rather flimsy, 'chicken-coops' of wood and canvas, capable of doing 80km/h (50 mph) flat out. As for the few licensed pilots, in 1914 they were seen only as sportsmen, lucky enough to have the background which allowed them to indulge in their reckless hobby.

A new force

However, it soon became clear that planes were useful. In September 1914, a British plane gave General Gallieni vital information on the German advance at the Battle of the Marne. In the autumn, observers began to photograph enemy lines. Soon there were specialist squadrons for observation and bombing.

In 1914 bombs were thrown by hand, and sometimes bundles of thin steel darts were flung at enemy infantry. As technology advanced, it became possible to hit key enemy installations. In 1915, for example, the French bombed the German chemical plants of Ludwigshafen, and later the coal mines of the Saar and the Ruhr. In reply, the Germans bombed factories in northern and eastern France, and their giant airships were even able to attack London. The first planes were slow and vulnerable. Faster machines with better weapons were needed; fighter planes.

Knights of the sky

With their fast, powerful machines, the fighter squadrons were highly regarded by everyone. The pilots and their exploits were also widely known: in France, Pégod, who was killed in 1915; Guynemer, an officer in the famous group of Swans, downed after 54 'kills'; Fonck, who notched up 75 'kills' by the end of the war; in Britain, Ball; in Belgium, Coppens; in Germany, von Richthofen, the 'Red Baron'. Their faces were known to everyone, and their uniforms were covered with medals and decorations. When the pilot Nungesser entered Maxim's restaurant in Paris, the talking stopped as all eyes turned to look at him, and perhaps to try and count the palm leaves on his war cross.

These men were also famous for their feminine conquests and their pranks. One night when the flyer Navarre attended a show at the Paris Olympia, he found his seat claimed by a higher-ranking officer. The pilot simply grabbed him and hurled him over the balcony into the stalls. On the ground, they lived riotously; when they were in the air their lives often hung by a thread. Pilots had no parachutes; a careless moment or a jammed gun and death was certain. They formed a military aristocracy, like medieval knights. One pilot risked his life to throw a wreath from his plane in honour of the opponent he had killed. Fonck used to wait until the enemy pilot had seen him before beginning the fight.

These individuals preferred to go out hunting the enemy on their own, when the mood took them. However, in 1917 the Germans adopted new tactics. Lone Allied pilots on patrol ran into German Fokker planes in groups of eight to ten. Lone sorties became very rare, as numerical superiority always triumphed in the end.

By the end of the war, France had 8,000 pilots and 3,600 planes. More than 20,000 planes had been built since 1914. In those four years, flying progressed more than it had done in the fourteen years since the first trials in about 1900.

A German plane overflying a goods train

25

War in the East

Lawrence of Arabia was 28 when he began his mission. An archaeologist and Oriental linguist, and a British agent since 1914, he led the Arab rebellion against the Turks. As a colonel, in 1917–18 he won vital victories during the conquest of Palestine. But his dream of uniting the Arabs in one nation allied to Britain was to remain unfulfilled. He retired from public life, and was killed in a motorbike crash in 1935.

Ever since the beginning of the war, Wilhelm II had tried to drag Turkey into the conflict. He wanted to force Russia to have to fight on two fronts, and to threaten the Suez Canal, one of Britain's most vital supply routes.

The Dardanelles trap

After bombing Russia's Black Sea ports, the Turks entered the war on 5 November 1914. They attacked the Caucasus, forcing the ill-prepared Russian units to retreat in disorder. The Allies had to take action. Winston Churchill, the British First Lord of the Admiralty, put forward an adventurous plan, which involved capturing the straits into the Black Sea and bombarding Constantinople, the Turkish capital. On 18 March 1915, an Anglo-French naval squadron entered the Dardanelles and smashed the Turkish defences with its gunfire. But it then ran into floating mines moored in the straits. Three vessels were sunk and the rest of the fleet had to retire. The move had failed.

A month later the Allies tried to disembark on the Gallipoli Peninsula, south of Constantinople. Bad luck and incompetent leadership dogged the whole project. As soon as the heavy barges touched land, they came under fierce Turkish fire. The men of the expeditionary force, many of whom were

The Dardanelles in 1915. On a sun-parched beach, Allied soldiers land equipment. The Turkish lines are only a few hundred metres over the hill but, in spite of the danger, some of the men cannot resist the temptation to cool down in the sea.

from Australia and New Zealand, were pinned down on the beaches where they suffered terribly for eight months. Shells, disease and storms decimated their numbers and shattered morale. Forced to reimbark, some relanded at Salonika in Greece, a country which did not enter the war until 1916. The war between Turkey and Russia became horrendous. In February 1915, 30,000 Turkish soldiers froze to death in the Caucasus Mountains. In Armenia, the Turks murdered some 500,000 local people whom they suspected of pro-Russian sympathies.

War in the desert

To alleviate the Turkish threat to the Suez Canal, the British began a desert war. In November 1914 an Indian army was put ashore at the top of the Persian Gulf and began to conquer Mesopotamia. Supplied by a fleet of boats sailing up the River Tigris, and with 1,000 mules and 600 camels, the British advanced on Baghdad. But in November 1915 a Turkish counter-attack forced them to retreat into the town of Kut-al-Amara, where famine and cholera killed thousands of them. Baghdad was eventually taken only in March 1917.

In Arabia, Colonel T.E. Lawrence managed to incite the local Bedouin tribes to rebel against the Turks. Fluent in Arabic, he managed to gain the confidence of the Arab leaders, above all, that of Emir Faisal of Mecca. In return for his support, the British promised to create a large new Arab state with Faisal as its king. At the head of an Arab legion of 10,000 men, Lawrence harrassed the Turks, driving them out of the Hejaz. He then joined with the larger British force which had advanced from Egypt, and they marched victoriously on Jerusalem, taking it on 9 December 1917. However,

the unity with the Arabs did not last. While Lawrence was negotiating with the Arabs, Balfour, the British Foreign Secretary, promised the persecuted Jews of Europe a national home in Palestine. Moreover, in 1916 he signed an agreement with the French to divide the Turkish Middle East between them. The seeds of future conflict were thus sown.

Arrests of Armenians in a Turkish town in 1915. The road has been blocked at both ends, and armed soldiers are rounding up the inhabitants. Most of the Armenians arrested were massacred.

The World at War

The war made even the high seas unsafe. The seamen of a torpedoed schooner watch helplessly as it sinks beneath the waves.

At the start of the war, historians talked and wrote about the 'European war', but by 1915 they had revised their opinion and began calling it the 'World War'. Never before had war engulfed all five continents at the same time.

The search for allies

Both sides tried hard to get neutral countries to join them. Allies were needed to strengthen the overall war effort, increase the number of fighting men, divide the enemy's forces and cut their supplies. Enemy territories were promised to neutral powers if they joined the conflict. Thus Italy, though allied to the Central Powers before the war, changed sides and declared war on Austria-Hungary in 1915. She had been promised part of Tyrol, Istria and Dalmatia. Bulgaria joined Austria to crush Serbia in October 1915, because at that time the Austrians seemed likely to win. In 1916, Romania joined the Allies, but after a few days of fighting she herself was invaded.

Like the tentacles of an enormous octopus, battle trenches spread across mountains and plains, forests and deserts. Throughout the world, Europeans and their allies opposed each other in a war without mercy.

War under other skies

In Africa, the French and British, helped by native soldiers, chased the Germans from their bases in Togo and the Cameroons. In East Africa the German general Lettow-Vorbeck held out with 1,500 men against British, Belgian and Portuguese troops until the end of the war in 1918. Japan, Britain's eastern ally, seized the Chinese ports controlled by Germany in 1914. British and Japanese ships captured the German Pacific islands and took the inhabitants prisoner. Most important of all, Africa and Asia were huge reservoirs of men and raw materials for the French and British. In the trenches of northern France, it was common to find Gurkha regiments from Nepal, turbaned Sikhs from the Punjab, and Senegalese or Moroccan riflemen shivering with cold and fever. These troops were used mainly during the attacks. They were brave fighters in a war that was not theirs but which killed them in tens of thousands.

Essential provisions such as cotton, oil, tea and sugar-cane, as well as rare metals such as nickel, tungsten and manganese dug from colonial mines, enabled the Allies to continue the war. However the vast quantities needed by the French and British exceeded what their empires could supply, forcing

Europe to appeal to America to keep the conflict going. From the United States, Argentina and Brazil came wheat, horses, meat, steel and copper. Already involved economically, several South American states stumbled into the war when the United States took the lead by declaring war on Germany on 6 April 1917 and on Austria-Hungary on 7 December of the same year.

Austro-Hungarian troops bivouacking at the foot of the Carpathian Mountains in winter 1915.

Above: *Indo-Chinese riflemen in oriental uniform waiting to embark for Europe. Unlike African units at the front, these men were used mainly as an urban police force.*

Left: *A postcard drawn in 1915, when Italy entered the war. An Italian soldier is crossing the Austrian border waving a Savoyan flat bedecked with the Allied flags.*

Britain at War

For centuries, Britain's military power had rested on what was the world's foremost naval force, which protected both home and Empire.

Wearing his khaki uniform, the officer finished his speech to the applauding London crowd: 'Don't let the Germans get away with their crimes in Belgium! England is fighting for freedom! Join up before it is too late!' A few steps away, the posters outside the recruiting office drove home the same message: 'Your country needs you', 'Remember Belgium', 'Do your duty'. Yet the war had taken Britain by surprise. Very much concerned with the administration of her empire, before 1914 Britain had relied heavily on the Royal Navy for her defence. The fleet stood guard over the British Empire, ready to step in anywhere in the world.

Britain was one of the few European countries that had no compulsory military service. Yet from August 1914 to September 1915, she managed to enlist nearly two million men, a huge yet ultimately inadequate force. With the help of imperial units, and the

Some cavalry and infantry units marching with their mascot. The British volunteer army of 1914 was small, and in 1916 compulsory military service was introduced.

introduction of conscription, she was able to mount the great offensives on the Somme and in Flanders in 1916 and 1917 – costly battles which were no more decisive than the offensives in the Dardanelles or Mesopotamia. The losses were huge; half a million men were killed or wounded on the Somme alone.

'Business as usual'

In 1914 this slogan summed up the common view of British bankers and businessmen who saw the war as a transitory phase which must not be allowed to interfere with business; Britain was the world's leading economic power and must remain so.

However, the government required industry to produce more and more weapons, vehicles and machines. Stretched to the limit by these orders, firms could no longer manufacture and sell abroad the goods on which their name had depended. Raw materials

Ireland

On 24 April 1916, Irish separatists in Dublin rose against Britain. Occupying vital points in the city, they posted notices on public buildings announcing 'We will serve neither King nor Kaiser, but Ireland'. The British Army responded quickly and on 30 April the rebels, faced with tanks and guns, were crushed. The uprising and its subsequent bloody suppression cost 1,500 lives. It was also largely responsible for the fall of Asquith, who was replaced as British Prime Minister by Lloyd George in December 1916.

began to run out. To carry on, firms had to borrow or buy from neutral countries. Thus Britain became increasingly dependent on convoys from the United States. Nevertheless, by 1917 the general state of the country was less serious than that of France. Most people were not starving, and the war was not being fought on home territory. But because of the 'submarine menace', the British fleet was unable to protect the vitally important Atlantic sea-lanes.

Carrying a wounded man through the mud near Passchendaele in Flanders, 1917. The British offensive which began there in the summer of 1917 soon became bogged down. Autumn rain soaked the soil. 'The terrain has turned into a vast bog of liquid mud', observed Colonel Fuller, commander of the British armoured divisions. Weapons and motorized vehicles became utterly useless and supplies very difficult to obtain. Whole teams of mules and their drivers disappeared in this sea of mud. When General Haig called off the operation in mid-November, the British had lost 265,000 dead and wounded, and had gained only a few kilometres of quagmire.

War at Sea

A British warship keels over after being torpedoed. Members of the crew can be seen clinging desperately to the hull.

At the start of the war the Allies decided to blockade Germany. The British navy prevented the German fleet from leaving port, while on the high seas any vessel making for Germany was intercepted and searched, and often its cargo was confiscated, in breach of the international agreement on the freedom of the seas. With her supplies of oil, copper, wool and rubber severely limited, Germany was forced to impose strict rationing on its citizens. Neutral countries were far from happy with this situation; the United States and Scandinavian countries wanted to go on trading with the Central Powers. However, the Allies' needs were so great that the neutrals more than made up for the loss of the German market.

Wilhelm II responded to the blockade with submarine warfare. In February 1915, he declared the waters round the British Isles a 'war zone'. On 7 May, a German U-boat torpedoed the passenger liner *Lusitania*, causing the death of 1,200 people, among whom were about 100 Americans. This produced such a hostile reponse from the United States government that the German Admiralty was forced to limit the scope of its submarine warfare.

The Battle of Jutland

Throughout the war the Allies dominated the seas, and the German fleet was bottled up in its home ports. Only once did the German high seas fleet try to break out. In May 1916 Admiral von Scheer tried to lure British ships towards the bulk of the German forces and so destroy them. But the British Admiral Jellicoe had intercepted the Germans' telegraph signals, and met the enemy fleet near the tip of the Danish island of

Jutland. Capital ships fired on each other at a range of over 16 kilometres (10 miles). Losses on both sides were heavy: 14 British and 11 German ships were sunk. In the end the Germans withdrew behind a smoke screen and returned to base. The conflict had achieved very little; after the only major naval battle of the war, the Germans remained trapped in port. Only 'raiders' such as the *Möwe*, a small steamer armed with guns and torpedoes, broke the blockade to plunder in the South Atlantic from Brazil to Africa, sinking over 20 Allied vessels between 1915 and 1917.

Defeating the U-boats
Only the activities of the German submarines could seriously hamper the Allies. Admiral Tirpitz persuaded the Kaiser of the value of his U-boats, and on 9 January 1917 Wilhelm II declared that 'terror will now strike both the enemy and the neutrals!' Immediately Germany's 120 submarines began to cause havoc, sinking one out of every four ships sailing for Allied ports. Britain was seriously affected, as she depended heavily on the sea link with her colonies and the United States. In order to keep supplies coming, the Admiralty eventually decided to gather merchant

ships together in convoys protected by warships. French and British naval captains were sceptical; they were unwilling to play at being 'sheep dogs', and claimed that convoys would merely give the U-boats a bigger target. In fact, submerged U-boats were slow, difficult to handle and, above all, vulnerable to the recently developed depth charges which were launched by convoy escort vessels. The experiment worked; Allied losses fell and more U-boats were sunk. By the summer of 1917 the Atlantic route was safe again. The German submarine war had failed. Moreover, it had played an important part in bringing the USA into the war on the side of the Allies.

A French battleship on convoy duty in the Mediterranean.

A German U-boat refuelling at Kiel after a sortie into British waters. Fast and agile on the surface, submarines were slow when submerged, and the batteries which powered their electric engines lasted only a few hours.

Spies and Secret Agents

Posters like this appeared in all public places, asking people not to talk about the war.

Clinging to the guttering, her feet on the edge of the sill, the young woman was listening at the open window. Snatches of conversation floated out: '. . . 25° longitude . . . 45° from the Straits . . . in Spanish waters . . . dinghies . . .'. The voices faded and a door slammed; the conversation had ended. Moving slowly along the low wall, she returned to her room and sat down at the desk to write a simple letter to her sister. A few lines in invisible ink were enough to pass on the vital information she had just overheard. Allied Intelligence would be pleased with her, for it was now clear how the Germans were supplying arms to the Moroccan rebels.

War in the shadows

The aim of the secret services, set up by all countries long before the war was to find out what the enemy was up to. Men and women were therefore sent out to get hold of any information that might be of use to the military – preparations for offensives, troop movements, new weapons, the state of the enemy's morale, and political plans. Many different devices were used to conceal messages: glass eyes, hollow teeth, buttons cut in half, combs, postage stamps, shoe heels, hat-pins, belts and suit linings. Allied aeroplane pilots were sometimes asked to drop agents behind the German lines. They often had to be collected under enemy fire. Homing pigeons were frequently used to carry messages, but soldiers at the front soon got orders to shoot any bird they suspected might be a carrier. The men were only too pleased to supplement their normal rations!

Spy fever

After a time, people began to see spies everywhere, and spying became more dangerous. Coloured handkerchiefs left out to dry for several days were believed to be coded messages. A mother carrying a flickering candle to light her children upstairs to bed might be giving a signal. Perhaps a house standing unscathed amid the ruins could be a base for traitors. The whole of Europe was caught up. 'Be on your guard, the enemy is listening', read posters everywhere.

A German poster put up at Charleville in September 1915. It relates how two French spies had been dropped by plane, captured, and found guilty by a military court. They had been shot on 1 September.

'The enemy is listening, so be careful on the phone!' reads this poster aimed at German soldiers.

Left: *Mata-Hari whose real name was Margareta-Gertruida Zelle, pretended to be an Indian dancer, and frequently appeared in the nude. Her grace and beauty made her famous, and she mixed easily in German military and political circles. Approached by the French counter-espionage service, she eventually accepted a mission from them. However, she was held responsible for the capture of a French agent, was arrested in Paris on 13 February, and shot at dawn on 15 October 1917.*

Verdun

A French soldier wrote home to his wife from the battlefield of Verdun: 'You cannot imagine the landscape around us. Not one plant is left. Here and there a tree-stump is left rising sadly from a landscape consisting of thousands of shell craters. There are no trenches or parapets from which to get a bearing. I am one of a few isolated men, crouching several hundred metres west of Fort Vaux. There is no barbed wire between us and the Germans, for everything has been pulverized by the continual bombardment. Worse than the gunfire, the lack of supplies, or the fear of attack, is the foul and heavy stench that hangs in the air and gives us cramp in our guts. It makes you feel sick, and prevents you from eating and even drinking. We live in a huge mortuary. Only the disgusting blood-gorged flies and sleek fat rats seem to like it here. The whole place stinks of rotting corpses, all sorts of human garbage, dust from explosives, and gas. You might have heard of Dead Man, or Hill 304, la Caillette Wood, the village of Fleury, or of Death Gully. Try to imagine each crater occupied by a man like me, alone and cut off, often without orders, just hanging on . . . If you asked me how or why I do it, I couldn't tell you.'

Hell

When Eugène Boin wrote this letter in May 1916, the battle had been in progress for four months. After a massive bombardment, the Germans advanced from their trenches in the afternoon of 21 February. Their officers had told the men that nothing could stop them, and that once Verdun was taken France would plead for peace. During the first few days the Germans did advance quickly. Fort Douamont, a key point in the defences of Verdun, fell on 25 February. Joffre then appointed General Pétain to take command of the defence. Early in March, the Germans attacked once more, on a wider front. At the cost of huge losses, the French held their attackers about 6 kilometres (4 miles) from their goal. Every ruin, every trench was bitterly fought over. Pétain was continually asking for reinforcements, but Joffre would let him have only a few. He was planning a great July offensive on the Somme and wanted to keep his troops fresh. Attacks and counter-attacks went on into April and

May. In early June, despite fierce resistance, Fort Vaux had to surrender. The Germans were now only 3 kilometres (2 miles) from Verdun. The critical point of the battle had been reached. Each metre of ground was captured only with terrible losses. The small fort at Thiaumont changed hands sixteen times during June and July. The German general staff knew that time was against them, for the Allied offensive on the Somme had begun on 1 July. On 11 July, the Germans tried one final attack. It petered out on the slopes around Fort Souville.

In spite of all the fierce fighting, the French now had the upper hand, and they counter-attacked in October. The forts of Douamont and Vaux were recaptured, and almost all the ground lost since February was retaken.

Who had won? The French had held out despite tremendous losses, and they claimed victory. The Germans believed, with some justification, that they had bled the French army white; it would never recover from the wound inflicted at Verdun. In fact, death was the real victor. The biggest battle ever fought had cost 400,000 lives.

French soldiers charge across a shell-torn landscape to attack a German trench which the occupants have not even had time to prepare for defence. At the centre of the picture, an infantryman has been hit by a German bullet. In the foreground, a German soldier is sheltering behind a piece of armour plate with a hole in it for his rifle barrel.

Left: *Two aerial photographs of Fort Douamont; one in early 1916 and the other after its recapture by the French in October. Only the outlines remained. During the battle, some 20,000,000 shells exploded on the ground, about two per square metre.*

All traffic to and from Verdun had to pass along this single road from Bar-le-Duc. At the height of battle, a lorry passed along this 'Sacred Way' every 10 seconds. If a lorry broke down, the driver would push it into the ditch to avoid blocking the road.

The Dead and Wounded

While the soldiers struggled forward in an attack, a constant stream of wounded men made their way as best they could from the hell of the front line. Those unable to walk, often hit by burning splinters of steel, remained where they fell, waiting for help.

The agony of the wounded

Some wounded men remained lost for days in the no-man's land between the lines, groaning, screaming with pain, or praying for relief. They would cry out despairingly for their friends who could not get near them but who had to listen to their terrible drawn-out agony. Those who were lucky enough to be picked up had to face a long and painful journey. On a stretcher, wrapped in a groundsheet or simply slung across someone's shoulder, they would be carried to the field station, a few hundred metres behind the front. But even there, there was little relief from the hell of war.

Those beyond help were left lying outside. A chaplain might be present to give them a final blessing. For many of the fallen, lost in battle and their bodies unrecognizable, there were no graves to which the living could later come to pray.

The luckier cases were given first-aid and a tetanus injection, and then evacuated to a military hospital. For some, this meant a painful journey across France in a slow and poorly equipped train. After being operated on, they woke up in a huge dormitory filled with the groans from neighbouring beds, the coughing fits of gas victims, and the death-rattle of the dying. After the daily visit of the chief medical officer, the orderlies or nuns got on with nursing the wounded. Women from all walks of life volunteered to become nurses, doing what they could to relieve the immense mental and physical anguish of the wounded. They performed many tasks in addition to their medical duties, such as reading letters to those who had been blinded, or listening to a young conscript who had been shot to pieces, and had written to his fiancée telling her that they would not now be able to live together. As the war dragged on, medical practice had to adapt itself to previously unimagined situations. The rigidly-fixed procedures, regulations and outdated manuals of the hospitals were overwhelmed by more than twenty-one million wounded. Ambulances, hospitals and gifts multiplied due to private initiative. Surgical techniques and the work of health services made striking advances. Vaccination and greater care to prevent the spreading of infection saved countless lives.

Going back
The wounded suffered an appalling trauma of confusion, misery and agony. All through the horror of the operating theatres, the daily round of the surgeons, doctors and orderlies, and questionings, there was always at the back of their mind the haunting fear that one day they would have to return.

The losses being suffered at the front were so serious that every country needed all the men it could get. And so, many of the wounded, often only barely recovered, found themselves on their way back to war. Invalids and those severely gassed were not sent back. The others were examined after all too brief a period of convalescence, and, if found fit for service, were returned to their units.

On the way back from the front, British wounded meet a German prisoner; for a brief while their mutual pain and sorrow brings them together. A minor wound was seen as a reprieve, a guarantee of life at least for another month or even a year. But only those badly maimed or gassed were discharged.

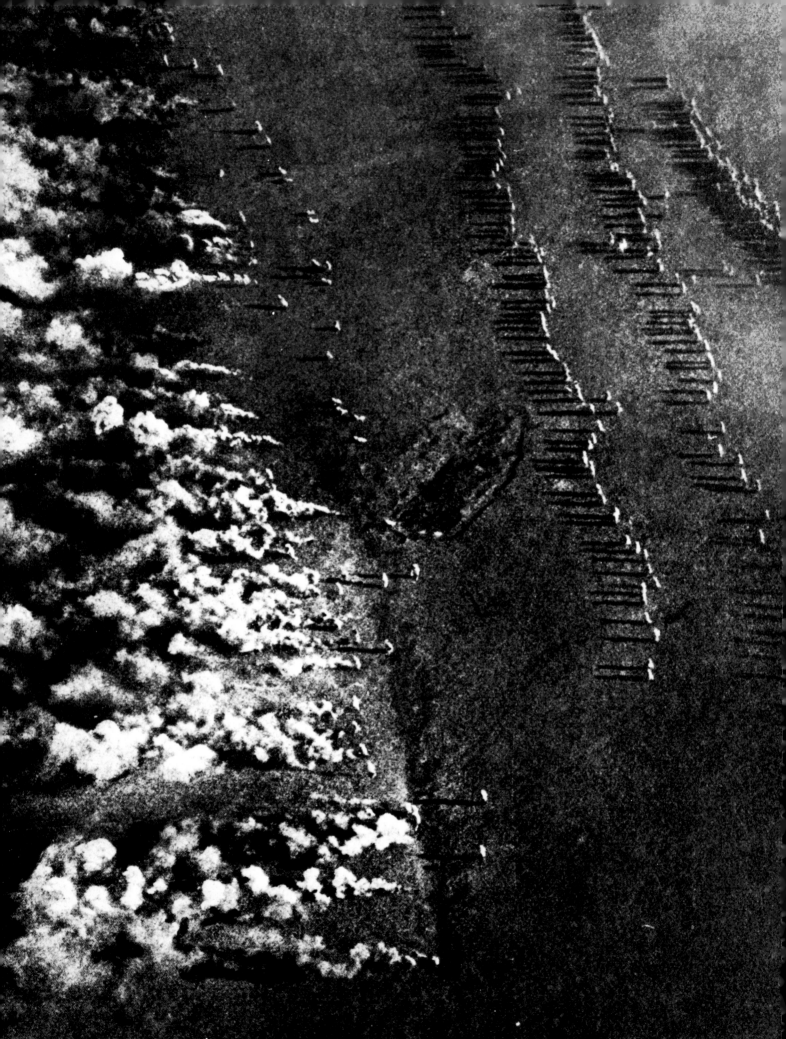

Machines of Death

From time immemorial, human beings have invented new, more efficient means of killing each other. The First World War was a time when they applied their wits and skill to the task of killing more than ever before. The strangest and craziest schemes were dreamed up and sometimes put into practice. In 1915 the Germans tried to make their planes invisible by using a kind of cellophane canvas. In Britain an explosive hook to fix on to enemy airships was invented. Some people wore medieval-style armour, such as helmets and cuirasses, and even devised shields on wheels behind which to advance. Some of the oddest ideas were for head-gear: a helmet which could be used as a bucket, pot or shovel; or a gun-hat which fired automatically but could also serve as a saucepan! Most of these devices stayed at the prototype stage, for they were too elaborate, costly or simply absurd. Regrettably, some new inventions were put to deadly use, most notably, poisonous gases, flame-throwers, and long-range guns.

War and technical progress

In other fields, great progress was made. Wireless technology made great headway, although the first sets were heavy and very bulky. As we have seen, surgery advanced spectacularly. However, the most decisive progress was made in the chemical industry. Cut off from their supply of raw materials by the naval blockade, Germany led in this 'laboratory war'. Their chemists developed substitutes from which they made explosives, paints, fertilizers, oil and fat, and they even tried to produce synthetic petrol from coal. All governments gave high priority to scientific research. A French staff officer wrote that 'at present, good laboratories are every bit as valuable as good divisions. Great chemists help us as much as great generals.'

A precursor of the modern aircraft-carrier: the deck of a British cruiser in 1918, adapted for carrying seaplanes which were used to protect convoys from German U-boats. The planes were lowered into the water to take off.

German soldiers practising with flame-throwers in 1916.

Opposite: *An aerial view of a German gas attack.*

The Home Front

This father of a large family came home on his first leave in 1915. These brief spells of respite allowed a farmer to take up a plough or scythe again, to relieve his wife of the heavy work that she had been doing in his absence. But within a few days, the soldier had to catch a train back to the front from which he might never again return.

In 1915, a cartoon in the Paris paper *L'Oeuvre*, showed two soldiers talking earnestly. 'Let's hope they'll hold out!', says one. 'Who?' 'The civilians, of course!'

For civilians, holding out meant living in a town or village without a priest or a teacher, and with nearly all men from 18 to 45 at the front. Communities were run by the elderly; women ploughed, mowed and harvested the fields. Every family dreaded hearing that a husband, son or brother had been killed in action. In the cities, goods were expensive, and obtainable only with rationing coupons. Huge German airships, called zeppelins, made bombing raids at night on people's homes. The optimistic reports in the newspapers differed dramatically from the cruel facts of front-line existence described in the soldiers' letters. Nonetheless thinking of those who were suffering in the trenches did help civilians to put up with all sorts of hardships in their own lives.

Drowning one's sorrows

Yet, even in war-torn France, life went on. The cafés and restaurants did not stand empty. Theatres, which had been closed in August 1914, soon opened their doors again. There were some who disapproved of this, asking 'How can you enjoy yourself while only 100 kilometres (60 miles) away other people are being killed?' However, shows were useful to keep up morale and amuse soldiers on leave or convalescing. Besides, in Paris alone the theatres employed thousands of people. Managers vied with each other in making generous gestures, donating 15 percent of their takings to charity or giving free shows for soldiers. The public soon forgot its scruples and returned to

Mistinguette, the unrivalled star of the Parisian 'café-concert' of the pre-war era, helped the war effort in her own way. Draped in the American flag, in the spring of 1917 she starred in a patriotic review about the glory of France's new ally.

the cinemas and café entertainments.

The atmosphere of pre-war Paris re-emerged. For a while patriotic shows topped the bill, but within a short space of time saucy and comic revues regained their popularity. Golden stripes and military helmets replaced the ostrich feathers of the dancing girls, but little else changed. Operettas were popular, some of them running for two years. Meanwhile, avant-garde artists exploded their own cultural 'bomb'. On 18 May 1917, the writer Jean Cocteau, the painter Picasso and the musician Erik Satie gave the première of their cubist ballet *Parade*. In the orchestra, sirens, whips and revolver shots could be heard; the clattering of a typewriter replaced the piano. On stage, strange and mottled figures indulged in grotesque contortions. In the audience were all the leading figures of Parisian society. Some people protested at what they regarded as an attempt to demoralize the nation. The evening ended in a riot. It was all excellent publicity!

Stories of the goings-on at home spread as far as the front line. Men on leave in Paris regarded those with jobs at home with bitterness. They were scornful and at the same time envious of them, calling them shirkers and cowards. Some soldiers, both officers and men, had found peaceful jobs as staff secretaries, drivers for generals or orderlies at the war ministry. Far from the battlefield, with its shells and trenches, they quietly sported their elegant uniforms in pavement cafés. Many soldiers at the front began to have doubts about what they were fighting for, and the sort of country they would find on their return.

The legendary calm of Londoners seemed little disturbed by zeppelin raids. A newspaper proudly announced that two of them had been brought down over the East coast.

In Paris, the pavement cafés on the great boulevards were crowded. The waiters of pre-war days were replaced by waitresses.

The Yanks are Coming!

Woodrow Wilson, the American president, constantly repeated his desire to stay out of a conflict that seemed of no concern to Americans. 'The European war is no business of ours,' he said, 'Neutrality is preferable to war . . .' However, the United States was the world's leading economic power, and so could not ignore the war. From the start, American industrialists and farmers exported their goods to the countries at war. Because of the blockade on Germany, they came mainly to Britain and France, who bought them on credit. Gradually American exporters realized that their debts would remain unpaid if the Allies were to lose the war. Journalists and senators felt that American intervention would prove decisive in the war. But, although the President might be won over, what about public opinion? Many Americans were of German origin.

What settled the matter was the submarine war. The United States could not see their ships being sunk and not react, especially as Germany had proposed to Mexico that she join Germany in a war against the States, and recapture Texas and New Mexico.

The might of America

The United States entered the war on 6 April 1917. 'The Yanks are Coming' ran a popular song of the time, reflecting the Allied optimism this provoked. However, declaring war is one thing, fighting it quite another. Money must be found, arms produced, volunteers trained, and ships and planes built. American industry set about its task with great vigour. The population threw itself into the war effort, subscribing to government loans and accepting days

I WANT YOU FOR U.S. ARMY
NEAREST RECRUITING STATION

without meat, or bread, to save these valuable foods. The results were astonishing: by the end of 1917, American shipyards could build a ship in just 25 days, and more ships were being launched than the Germans could sink. On 13 July 1917, the first American soldiers disembarked in the French port of Boulogne, which was bedecked with American flags to mark the occasion. The local crowd could hardly believe their eyes; sun-tanned, clean-shaven, in spotless khaki uniforms and wide-brimmed scout hats, a troop of athletes jumped ashore shouting and laughing. How different they were from the war-weary men returning from the front. In Paris, journalists besieged the hotel where General Pershing was staying. Newspapers spoke of the 'great friendship between our nations, united forever by their love of freedom'. The belief was that the Americans would swiftly finish off the German army and that arms, supplies and food would begin pouring into Europe. The reality was different. By the end of 1917, only 175,000 Americans had disembarked. They were badly prepared for trench warfare and equipped with unsuitable or even useless weapons. Foch wanted to absorb the Americans into his own forces as they arrived, but Pershing objected. He insisted on keeping command of an independent American army which he would take to the front as soon as it was strong enough. In the end, however, American participation was to give the Allies a decisive advantage.

Wilson's Fourteen Points

On 8 January 1918, even before American units had entered the fray, in a speech to Congress President Wilson had set out his plans for the future peace. He sought to satisfy the Allies' war aims, but he also wanted European borders

redrawn to suit the needs of national minorities. He planned that colonial questions would be settled in the interests of the native populations, and that worldwide disarmament be organized. Above all, he wished to set up a League of Nations which would include all states and thus make future war impossible.

Top: *A requisitioned steamer which has been turned into a troopship disembarks an American company and all its gear at Saint-Nazaire.*

Above: *The Americans played a vital part in the second Battle of the Marne in the summer of 1918.*

1917, Year of Discontent

The blast of an exploding shell has just killed two more men on the Russian front. Everywhere, this scene was repeated thousands of times. At home as much as at the front, weariness turned to anger, as each battle was seen as senseless butchery. Mutinies and suicides among the soldiers also increased.

In January 1917, queues stretched in front of bakeries in cities all over mainland Europe. In Berlin, the authorities gave out firewood in exchange for potato peelings, which chemical factories were able to turn into fertilizer. In Paris, women frantically searched rubbish heaps to find a few pieces of coal. All the countries at war faced a serious political and economic crisis as prices rose faster than wages. Discontent grew and strikes, at first rare and scattered, became more numerous. They hit German steelworks and French textile mills, banks and even armaments factories, where women workers began to take industrial action. Governments reacted by giving a few pay rises, moving strike leaders to other factories and sending some 'trouble-makers' to the front. Above all, they tried to prevent riots, like the one in Turin, in Italy, which nearly turned into a revolution.

People everywhere were fed up with the war. They had been told it would be over in two months. It had already lasted more than three years. They wanted no more young men killed and maimed for no apparent reason. They craved peace. What was the point of all these sacrifices? Why not just call an armistice?

The idea gained ground on both sides. In France, Joseph Caillaux, former President of the Council lent his support to it. In Germany, socialist deputies asked parliament to seek a 'peace of mutual understanding in which each side would renounce its conquests'. Charles I, who had succeeded Franz Joseph to the Austro-Hungarian throne in 1916, knew that his country was holding on only with German help. In the spring of 1917, he tried to open secret negotiations with France. In August, Pope Benedict XV appealed to both sides for a cease-fire. But nothing came of it, as nobody was willing to give in. The war certainly no longer had unanimous support, and there were even hostile demonstrations. In southern Italy, crowds of women had gathered shouting 'Down with the war! Give us back our men!' Many French and German socialists wanted to follow the example of the Russian Revolution and lead the workers in a great movement to transform society.

To the bitter end!

However, nationalism and the desire for victory were too strong. Georges Clémenceau, aged 76, resumed the presidency of the French Council in November 1917. His policy was simple: total war. In Britain and Italy, Lloyd George and Orlando also managed to ensure that the war would be continued until they had complete victory. Censorship was stepped up and the courts punished pacifists heavily. By the end of 1917, only Russia had pulled out

'All items made of aluminium, copper, brass, nickel and tin are reusable', proclaims a German poster. The poster's red stripe meant that it had to be displayed in all collecting centres.

of the conflict, having lost millions of men in the fighting, and undergone a revolution. Freed from threats in the east, Germany and Austria were now able to throw all their might into the battle on the western front. The year of 1918 was to be decisive.

In the rue du Faubourg Saint-Denis in Paris, an endless queue has formed following the announcement that some coal has arrived at the merchant's. The news soon spread through the whole neighbourhood. Housewives waited several hours in the open air to get 5 to 10 kilos (11–22 lbs) of fuel, enough to keep a stove alight for barely two days.

Before 1917, mass mutinies were rare, but refusal to obey orders did occur. Even in trivial cases, courts martial passed savage sentences as an example to others. Here a mutineer is being executed by firing squad.

Mutiny

General Pétain visiting the front in the summer of 1917.

'Look at this lads, we're being sent into the attack!'

'Not again! We've only been in the second line for three days, and they promised us three weeks off!'

'See for yourself. Here it is in black and white: attack the Craonne plateau, dated 10 May 1917.'

'It can't be true, we've already lost 600 men on the barbed wire, and we only have 2,000 in the regiment . . . and this is the third time we've been sent up front!'

'That's right, we've been in the firing line from the start. Why is it always us?'

'I agree. We've had enough. We'll go up to the front, but we won't join the attack! It's a waste of men.'

'You're mad. You're talking mutiny; we'll all be shot.'

'I don't care. We'll all be killed anyway, here or up there, sooner or later . . . we're expendable.'

Standing around in the mud, the restless and angry soldiers yelled at their officers who came to collect them. They wouldn't move, refusing to go up to the front. 'Down with war! Long live peace!', they shouted.

Early in May 1917, revolt was widespread among the French infantry. Groups of soldiers refused to obey orders, some demanded that hostilities stop. The authorities viewed this very seriously, the generals imagining it to be part of a plot hatched at home by revolutionaries. General Franchet d'Esaperey wrote: 'It is organized in Paris and, with German backing, it is trying to deliver France into the hands of the enemy.' 'We must hunt out those who are spreading this indiscipline', President Poincaré asserted.

Saving blood

As they blamed this crisis on subversive leaders and on pacifist propaganda, the authorities did not bother to find out its true causes. Ever since 1914, offensives had multiplied, piling up the casualties but with no gains to show. The last one, on the Chemin des Dames in April and May, was yet another bloody failure: soldiers attacking the Craonne plateau were simply cut down by German machine-guns. This was the last straw! The infantry went up to the front line but refused to join in an attack which they regarded as criminal folly. General Pétain was one of the few who understood what the men felt. 'The malaise is deeply rooted, but can be dealt with,' he told the President on being appointed to lead the French army on 15 May 1917. Although he had about 50 of the mutineers executed, he also made the soldiers' lives more bearable. More leave was granted, and more regularly, and the soldiers' resting quarters were improved. His main aim, however, was to save lives.

No longer were men sent against machine-guns, and costly local attacks were stopped. He summed up his policy as 'artillery conquers, infantry occupies'. From early summer, these measures began to show results. Gradually the mutinies died down and then stopped altogether. Army morale rose; the crisis was over.

An example of a tract written by mutineers, calling on others to join their revolt. Those found distributing such leaflets risked being court-martialled.

Although Clémenceau believed in fighting to the finish, he also knew how to gain popularity with the soldiers, and he helped to restore order in the army.

49

Revolution in Russia

Tsar Nicholas II, in the summer of 1917, a prisoner of the revolutionaries. Less than a year later he and his entire family were murdered.

Riots in Petrograd, July 1917. The crowd on Nevski Prospekt scatters as Kerensky's soldiers open fire.

Petrograd, Sunday 11 March 1917. Nearly 200,000 demonstrators had crowded on to Nevski Prospekt, waving placards and banners which read: 'Down with the aristocracy! We want bread!' Facing them were the Tsar's soldiers with a machine-gun at the ready, waiting for orders.

The end of Tsarism

At his headquarters, Nicholas II wanted to crush the revolt whatever the cost. However, he failed to understand that the Russian people, who had suffered unbearably, had nothing left to lose. They were dying of hunger in the big cities, while tonnes of food were rotting on Siberian railway stations because there were no lorries or trains to transport it. The government could not control the crisis; they wanted to strengthen the country through war, but they only succeeded in pushing people deeper into misery. Nicholas ordered that the riots in the capital be put down. On Nevski Prospekt, the order came 'Fire! In the name of the Tsar!' Not a shot was heard. The soldiers ran forward and mingled with the demonstrators; their officers were disarmed and some of them were shot. The government could no longer rely on the support of the army. Throughout Petrograd, soviets (councils) of workers and soldiers sprang up, replacing the government. Deputies from the *Duma* (Russia's parliament) formed a provisional government. The Tsar, recognizing that his regime had collapsed, abdicated on 17 March 1917.

War or peace

Although they had united to topple the Tsar, the revolutionaries were divided over what policies to pursue. In the central soviet of Petrograd, hardline socialists like Trotsky wanted to go so far

as setting up a state-controlled economy, and nationalizing the banks, factories and all land. Above all they wanted to make peace with the Central Powers. The Germans saw a way to profit from the situation. In April they allowed Lenin, head of the Bolshevik party and an advocate of immediate peace, to leave his exile in Switzerland, cross Germany and reach Russia.

The provisional government of moderate socialists, the most well-known, among whom was the lawyer Kerensky, was opposed to radical revolution. They put their hope in a military offensive that would evoke an outburst of patriotic feeling. For a while, the Allies were relieved that Russia would stay in the war. However, in summer 1917 the position worsened, and on the Russian front soldiers deserted in droves. In July, 500,000 people gathered on the Nevski Prospekt in a premature Soviet revolution. 'Down with war! Let Kerensky have the first bullet! All power to the soviets!' The army opened fire and a number of people were killed. Kerensky outlawed the Bolsheviks, and Lenin had to flee to Finland.

All power to the Bolsheviks!
However, by the autumn the situation in Russia was more propitious for a second revolution. The Bolsheviks were strong on the Petrograd soviet. Lenin gave the signal to begin, and on 6 November Bolshevik guards occupied strategic points all over the capital.

Kerensky had no choice but to flee. Power was now in the hands of Lenin and the Bolsheviks. At once they decided to stop the war: the country could not continue with it anyway, with no organized army or supplies. A cease-fire was signed with the Central Powers in December. After three months of negotiations, peace was concluded at

Brest Litovsk, in March 1918. Huge areas of Russia were handed over to the Germans, and the Bolsheviks agreed to pay enormous reparations, and supply Germany with wheat. The Allies were greatly disturbed. With peace in the east, the Germans and Austrians could now move millions of men to the western front. Moreover, Ukrainian wheat would undermine their naval blockade. And perhaps the disease of revolution might spread westwards from Russia. The 1917 revolution not only altered Russia; it also changed the war.

Top: *Lenin addressing a crowd from an improvized platform, during the summer of 1918.*

Above: *A soldiers' soviet displaying the red Communist flags, posed for this picture a few days after the Revolution. Officers and men were united by the same revolutionary ideals.*

Tanks

For the German soldier Helmut Müller, stationed near Cambrai, 20 November 1917 began like any other day. He had retired to the second line three days ago. He could hear the thunder of guns from the front line, but there seemed to be no immediate danger. However, the noise seemed to be getting closer. Suddenly a group of terrified soldiers appeared, fleeing in disarray from the front line. What on earth could produce such fear in men hardened by three years of trench warfare? Then Helmut saw it. A steel monster appeared out of the mists, crushing everything in its path, advancing on him and spitting fire from its two cannons and four machine-guns. He dived into a shell-hole, and hid his face in the mud, his

hands over his helmet. He knew he must be about to die. But nothing happened, except that there was a lot of rattling and the noise of an engine receding into the distance. What he had seen was one of the 375 British Mark IV tanks which that morning had launched the first great tank attack in history.

False starts

During 1915, both French and British general staffs had toyed with the idea of armoured cars. Large pieces of artillery, weighing over 7 tonnes, were slow and difficult to move using horses. Therefore, they were mounted on tractors with steel caterpillar tracks. This enabled them to advance in mud and climb steep slopes. On 1 February, the

The French Saint Chamond tank was first used in the 1917 offensive at the Chemin des Dames. Too unwieldy, badly designed and poorly handled, almost all of them were destroyed by German artillery.

British Mark I tank was shown to the authorities. Some months later it was issued to the Royal Tank Corps engaged on the Somme. The results were disappointing. Once the surprise had worn off, these 23-tonne mastodons became easy prey for artillery. They could advance at only 3km/h (2 mph), and as they carried less than 340 litres (80 gallons) of fuel their range was only about 25km (15 miles). They could be stopped by a simple ditch in front of the trenches, and then they became stationary targets. Shells pierced the thin protective plate easily and their crews of eight usually perished, roasted alive by exploding fuel.

Two British despatch riders on motorbikes, which gradually replaced horses and bicycles.

A decisive weapon

Although the British breakthrough on 20 November went deep into enemy territory, it fizzled out after 15 hours. On the 21st, several German divisions launched a counter-attack. In holding the ground won by the tanks the British lost 43,000 men; the Germans suffered 41,000 casualties. 'What use are tanks?', asked von Maritz, the German general commanding this sector. His general staff agreed with him. However, General Pétain had faith in them, and asked for a small, light machine to be developed to accompany attacking infantry. The tank was to be a shield behind which men could shelter as they advanced. It had to be fast and manoeuvrable. So the FT17 was developed by Louis Renault in his factories at Billancourt. It weighed 5 tonnes, against the 20 tonnes of other tanks. It moved at 8km/h (5 mph), and was less vulnerable. The crew comprised one driver, and a gunner sitting in the turret behind a 37mm cannon and a machine-gun. Almost 3,000 of these tanks were made and, from July 1918, they played a vital part in the eventual Allied victory.

A German A7V tank, a few of which were built by Daimler in Berlin. First used in March 1918, there were never enough of them to play an important part in the war.

The first British-made armoured cars. Called 'tanks', to mislead any possible enemy spies, they fought in pairs; one carried a cannon, the other only machine-guns.

The Last Offensive

Emerging from a cloud of gas, a German assault section goes into the attack. These crack troops were carefully selected and led by fiercely determined officers.

In January 1918, the German field marshals Ludendorff and Hindenburg were studying the map of Europe. They knew that although peace with Russia was imminent, the Americans would soon be at the western front in force. Germany had to strike before the summer; any delay and it would be too late. However, they had no new weapons, only a few more heavy guns than the Allies, and above all they had only a tenth of the number of tanks. New tactics were devised: stun the enemy lines with a short, accurate and extremely heavy artillery bombardment, then follow with waves of élite assault troops, closely supported by squadrons of bombers.

Thunder on the Somme

The spot they chose for the attack was a weak link in the front where the French

and British armies met on the Somme. At 5 a.m. on 21 March 7,000 guns signalled the start of the offensive. The British were paralysed and fell back, and the German infantry rushed into the gap. Within four days they had advanced 22 kilometres (14 miles). The war of

Kaiser Wilhelm II during the German 1918 offensives

54

movement had returned. The British commander, General Haig, feared the worst and agreed to place all Allied troops under a single commander-in-chief. The job went to General Foch. When Clémenceau congratulated him, the general replied: 'A nice present! You hand me a lost battle and ask me to win it!' Yet at the cost of 250,000 casualities the French and British managed to close up the front again. The Germans had suffered equally heavy losses. To make up for them, the politicians sent boys aged 17½ and men of 50 to the front.

On 24 March, Parisians received the first shells from 'Big Bertha', the huge German guns hidden in the forest of Saint-Gobain, 110 kilometres (70 miles) from the capital. During the blind bombing of houses and monuments, a single shell fell on the church of Saint-Gervais killing 80 people at mass.

On 9 April, a new offensive rocked the Flanders front but failed to breach it. Then, on 27 May, achieving total surprise, the Germans attacked the Chemin des Dames and pushed the French back to the River Aisne; on 1 June they reached Château-Thierry only 90 kilometres (56 miles) from Paris. As in the dark days of 1914, the capital was threatened, and its fate was once more to be decided on the Marne.

Opposite Ludendorff, Pétain was determined to hold out at any cost. On 15 July fifty-two German divisions ran into fierce resistance between Soissons and Reims. Allied planes controlled the skies and shot down the enemy's crucial observation balloons. The Americans prevented the Germans from settling on the left bank of the Marne. Foch now decided that the time had come to counter-attack. For some days, without the Germans knowing, his troops and tanks had been assembling in the forest of Villers-Cotterêts. On 18 July, ten divisions and 400 tanks attacked the enemy's flank. Taken completely by surprise, the Germans were forced to retreat; this was the end of German hopes and from that point onwards the Allies remained on the offensive. Victory seemed inevitable.

Left: *One of the guns that bombarded Paris from March to August 1918. Of the 367 shells which it fired, one caused the massacre in the church of Saint-Gervais, whose battered nave is shown above. These guns, named 'Big Bertha' by the Parisians, had a 30-metre (100-ft) barrel, and could hurl a 120-kilogramme (265-lb) shell a distance of 120 kilometres (75 miles). All the documents about them were destroyed, so we will never know how German engineers had managed to cast such monsters.*

Facing Defeat

An 18-year-old German prisoner in 1918

The German offensive in Champagne had failed, and Germany and her allies were exhausted. The armies of the Central Powers had run out of manpower. The balance now tipped in favour of the Allies, and the intervention of the United States proved decisive. Over a million American soldiers were now based in France. On all fronts, the Allied forces were superior to those of the Germans in both numbers and equipment.

The final attack
The Allies decided to push on with the offensive. Foch wanted to hammer the German front without pause, gradually forcing the enemy to retreat. On 8 August 1918 the Germans in Picardy fell back, 'A black day for the German army', wrote Ludendorff. German morale was indeed low: 'Down with strike-breakers. Down with those who prolong war!', soldiers shouted at units arriving to reinforce the line. American and French divisions entered Lorraine on 12 September. At the end of the month, a general offensive was launched along the whole front. The Germans attempted by every possible means to delay the Allied advance, but were pushed back. On 8 October, the British entered Cambrai. A week later German troops left the Belgian coast. Even more worrying to the German general staff was the fact that their Turkish and Bulgarian allies were on the verge of collapse.

The fall of empires
In the Balkans, Bulgarian troops were defeated by the French and Serbians at the end of September, and on the 27th, Bulgaria surrendered unconditionally. In Palestine, the British Army broke through the Turkish lines, and on 26 October it marched on Constantinople. Four days later the Turks signed an armistice. At the same time, the Hapsburg Empire fell apart. The Czechs, Poles and Hungarians established provisional governments to negotiate with the Allies. Whole army divisions simply abandoned the front line. On 23 October, the Italians launched an offensive at Vittorio Veneto on the River Piave. Half a million Austrian soldiers were captured and their Hungarian allies drifted away from the front. On 3 November, Charles I, the Hapsburg emperor, signed an armistice with the Italians.

In spite of these setbacks, the German general staff were determined to hold out to the bitter end. The government in

Berlin tried to win time by negotiating directly with the United States on the basis of the 'Fourteen Points' which President Wilson had suggested in January 1918 as a list of war aims and plans for the post-war organization of Europe. However, while Germany tried to stem the Allied advance in the west, revolt was brewing at home. When it was announced on 29 October that the navy was going to leave port on a sortie, German sailors mutinied. They joined with the workers from the naval arsenal at Kiel. Many crews were won over by socialist propaganda and joined the revolt. On 4 November, the port was completely in the hands of a sailors' soviet. Revolution spread quickly to the large cities, and on 5 November the red flag flew over Berlin and Munich. The government was helpless; it had no reliable troops it could call upon for assistance. The mutineers now controlled strategic points in the railway network and threatened to starve the army at the front into submission.

Right: *For the first time since 1914, fighting once more took place in open country. Here two Frenchmen are defending a position with a machine-rifle.*

Autumn 1918. American troops advancing to the front, supported by Renault tanks.

Americans liberating a village on the Meuse. For this elderly couple, four years of German occupation are now at an end.

The Armistice

The car of the German delegation crossing the French lines to receive the terms of the armistice.

The evening of 7 November 1918 was foggy. A car with a large white flag moved slowly forward; inside were a German minister and three soldiers. When they arrived at the French lines they were led to the station at Tergnier, from where a special train took them to Compiègne. Foch received them at once. 'What are your terms, Marshal?' the German minister asked. 'I am allowed to tell you only if you have come here for an armistice,' replied Foch. 'Is that what you want?' After a brief consultation, the Germans answered, 'Yes'.

The Death of a Poet

Wilfred Owen, one of the finest British poets of the century, was killed in action in France a week before the armistice in 1918. In *Dulce et Decorum Est* he expressed vividly his disillusionment with the war:

> My friend, you would not tell with such high zest
> To children ardent for some desperate glory,
> The old lie: Dulce et decorum est
> Pro patria mori.

(The Latin in the last two lines means 'How sweet and lovely it is to die for one's country'.)

The carriage at Rethondes

A document was handed to them at once. The conditions were punitive. Germany was to evacuate the left bank of the Rhine, and surrender all her guns, machine-guns and submarines; the blockade was to remain in force, and the Allies would retain control of their enemy's supplies. The German delegation was given three days to consider the terms. During this time, the fighting went on, and soldiers continued to be killed and wounded.

Meanwhile, power was changing hands in Germany. The Kaiser wanted to fight on. He would take command of the army personally and, if necessary, plunge the country into civil war. But his generals forced him to abdicate. To prevent the Spartakists (the German Bolsheviks) from seizing power in Berlin, moderate socialists proclaimed a republic and formed a provisional government. On 11 November, at 5.10 a.m. in Foch's carriage standing in a clearing at Rethondes, the Germans signed the armistice. In the front line near Mons at 10.50 a.m., a British lieutenant saw a German soldier appear unarmed and without his helmet. He was drunk with joy, 'The war is over! OVER!' The lieutenant thought he was mad. In the German trenches, however, rumours had spread and soldiers brought out red flags and republican cockades, ready to fraternize with the enemy. But their officers, with revolvers drawn, threatened the leaders. The fighting might resume any moment! But, the news was confirmed, and all along the front the call for a cease-fire sounded. The worst carnage the world had ever known had finally come to an end.

Relief

Bells were rung all over Europe. In the capital cities, no one slept that night. In Paris, strewn with Allied flags, a million people took to the streets, embracing, singing, dancing and carrying soldiers in triumph. Parisians wanted to forget four years of nightmare. In Berlin, too, they celebrated the armistice. The feeling of relief was stronger than the bitterness of defeat, particularly as their soldiers had not been beaten. At the time of the cease-fire they were still occupying parts of France. In a speech to the French parliament, Clémenceau summarized the situation: 'Yes, we have won the war and not without great effort. Now we must win the peace, and that may well be more difficult.'

This German poster calls on rebel sailors to remember their basic civil duties: 'Comrades, take care! Preventing the movement of goods causes starvation!'

Above: *In Budapest on 29 October 1918, the public applaud truckloads of soldiers as they career down the street. The Hapsburg Empire had collapsed.*

The Place de l'Opéra in Paris on 11 November 1918. The joy and relief of the Parisians are plain to see.

The Lost Peace

In Paris on 18 January 1919, a crowd of curious people gathered near the Foreign Ministry, where the peace conference was about to open. One after the other, the Allied representatives were applauded as they arrived. Lloyd George of Britain, Orlando of Italy and, above all, the American President Wilson whose Fourteen Points, formulated a year earlier, were to serve as the basis for the settlement. A great roar greeted the arrival of Clémenceau. An icy silence marked the entrance of the Germans. They were not there to negotiate, but to obey the will of the victors.

The Treaty of Versailles

On 28 June, in the Hall of Mirrors of the Palace of Versailles, where Wilhelm I had proclaimed the German Empire in 1871, Clémenceau opened the ceremony of signing the most important of all the treaties. Germany, who alone was held responsible for the war, had to pay for the destruction. In future, her army would be limited to 100,000 men, with no tanks, heavy guns or planes. Alsace-Lorraine was to be returned to France. Germany's colonies were taken away, and the country was cut in two by the Danzig corridor, which gave the newly reconstituted state of Poland access to the Baltic Sea. The Treaty of Versailles, and the peace treaties signed subsequently with Austria, Bulgaria, Hungary and Turkey, changed the face of Europe. New states emerged from the remains of the dismantled Hapsburg Empire. Most of them comprised people of different nationalities, among whom were many Germans who now found themselves under the authority of the Czechs, Poles, or Hungarians. Some decided to emigrate to Germany or Austria; others stayed but formed political parties with which to fight their

new masters. As soon as the treaties were signed they were challenged by force. In Poland in 1919, the Red Army tried to take Warsaw. In Turkey in 1922, General Mustafa Kemal overthrew the Sultan and drove the Greeks from land which the Treaty of Sêvres had given them two years earlier.

Many Germans rejected the peace terms. 'After all, our army was not defeated!' In Munich, a recently demobilized corporal held several meetings in which he denounced the 'Diktat' of Versailles. His name was Adolf Hitler. Neither were all the victors satisfied with the treaties. The Italians had not got the land they wanted, and a coup led by ex-soldiers and directed by the nationalist poet Gabriele D'Annunzio, led to the occupation of the Yugoslavian city of Fiume, where many Italians lived. Benito Mussolini attacked Allied policy and established the first

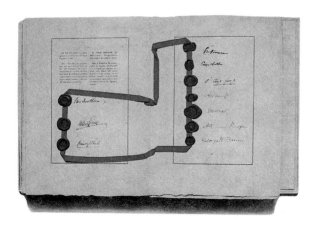

The last page of the treaty of Versailles, signed and sealed by the negotiators. This is a photograph taken in 1920 of the original document, which disappeared from the archives during the German occupation of France in the Second World War.

Fascist party to take power in post-war Europe. The peace was criticized from all sides. However, the Allies were too divided among themselves to solve the problems. The strongest of them, the United States, lost interest in Europe altogether. Congress refused to ratify the treaties when the League of Nations, charged with keeping the peace, held its first sessions. The peace had already been lost.

On 14 July 1919, Marshals Foch and Joffre led the victory parade along the Champs Élysées. Parisians applauded the victors as they passed, relieved at the end of a conflict which was described as 'the war to end all wars'.

The End of the World

Berlin in 1918. An invalided ex-officer forced to resort to begging to survive. Five years earlier, Prussian officers had been among the pillars of the German Empire. The war had ruined them. Their wealth had passed into the hands of war profiteers, for whom the conflict had been just a means of getting rich quickly.

Ten million dead, six million invalids; over twenty million killed and wounded in all. In France, Italy, Russia and the Balkans, hundreds of thousands of houses, farms and factories lay in ruins; millions of hectares of agricultural land was unusable; whole merchant fleets had been virtually wiped out; trade links had been broken. This was the appalling cost of the Great War.

Europe in ruins

In 1919, Europe was almost totally ruined. Germany was crippled by having to pay heavy 'reparations'. The governments of France, Britain and Italy had borrowed vast sums of money from their citizens and, above all, from the United States. Their treasuries were empty. During the war, they had conducted almost no trade. Japan, which had played only a small part on the Allied side, and the United States, which had come in late, had displaced them all over the world, cornering the markets for foreign trade.

The true victor of the war was the United States. By 1919 they owned half the world's gold, their factories were the most up-to-date, and their merchant fleet was one of the world's largest. Prices in Europe went on rising while wages remained stagnant, and many people saw their income dwindling. On the other hand there were some who had amassed colossal fortunes in the armaments industry or military supply. The brash behaviour of these 'war profiteers' and the speed at which they had made their fortunes was shocking to many.

The roaring twenties

The war had upset many social patterns. The place of women in work had changed, as had attitudes towards morality. Enforced separation had destroyed many marriages, and numerous families had broken up. Almost an entire generation of young men had been wiped out. Those soldiers who did survive to return to civilian life soon realized that they had come back to a different world from the one they had left. Faced with competition for jobs from women and even German prisoners, many ex-soldiers remained unemployed and had to resort to begging. Because these wounded, mutilated and disfigured men reminded people all too sharply of the war, they were often treated with indifference. The Russian Revolution offered a vision of hope for some of these disillusioned soldiers. Between December 1918 and December 1919, the Spartakists tried to impose Communism on the new German republic. In Hungary, a rebel government took power from April to July 1919. In Moscow, the Bolsheviks tried to organize world revolution and set up an 'International' that was to gather together Communists from all countries. They also encouraged colonial peoples to revolt against their masters. For their part, the European governments severely repressed the Communists whom they vilified as 'men with knives between their teeth'.

In everything it did, Europe had only one aim: to forget the war and its hardships. Many of those who could afford it devoted themselves to sensual pleasure, to dancing and night-clubs. To others, the injustice of the post-war world was unbearable. There were long and bitter strikes which degenerated into violent confrontations. The confidence of Europe in her 'civilization' had been smashed by the mass slaughter of the First World War.

The town of Arras seen from a plane in 1918. Although some distance from the front, the town had been subjected to almost continuous German gunfire, and had been virtually destroyed. Of the houses which remained standing, few had a roof. Who was to pay for all the damage? In France, there was only one answer: 'Germany will pay!'

Women at War

Women servicing a locomotive in a French railway depot

fumes. Women repeatedly came into contact with harmful materials such as lead, copper and nickel. The oil which squirted from machinery caused skin diseases – 'oil spots'. Those who had to measure out certain acids became known as the 'canary crew' because the chemicals gave them a lemon-yellow complexion. Often exhausted, and working in unhygienic conditions, they were frequently involved in accidents, and contracted infectious diseases such as tuberculosis. In France, pregnant women were, in fact, exempt from night work, but the ante-natal rest period of 4 weeks, allowed to them from

'Verin Hector, gone off with the 3rd Dragoons, leaves his wife and children in the care of his neighbours.' This astonishing inscription could be seen on walls in Paris in August 1914. It illustrated an age-old male attitude, that women were lost without men! Women, of course, could manage on their own, but they experienced great anguish when they suddenly became totally responsible for their families. Within a few months, members of the 'weaker sex' had taken on almost all the tasks previously reserved for men.

Munition girls and dock lasses
Language and street scenes were both changing. New names were coined for all sorts of jobs which women were now doing instead of men. Waitresses were 'nippies', and bus conductresses 'clippies'. In the country, women helped by children and the elderly did the sowing, harvesting, and stacking of the crops; and some even pulled ploughs when there were no draught animals. In armaments factories, there were more and more munition girls. From 1916 onward, it was forbidden to employ workers who could be called up in jobs that could be done by women. 'If all the women factory workers stopped for twenty minutes, the Allies would lose the war', said General Joffre. However, the work was hard; women laboured for 12, 13 and sometimes 14 hours a day, day and night and even on Sundays, for pay that was usually lower than that of men in the same jobs. Most of the work was unhealthy, in dusty factories filled with gas and toxic

In the Berlin streets road works were left to women, but the police were still men!

1917 onwards, was often shamefully shortened or even cancelled. There were meant to be feeding rooms for women with babies but few firms provided them. Owners preferred the cheaper solution of allowing mothers to use a room such as a porter's lodge, a refectory or a store room. After the war ended, the men returned to their former places, and the women to theirs. But how things had changed! Women in short skirts, silk stockings and with their hair cut short; these were not the same women who had wept as their men left for the front in 1914. In four years, the women of France, Britain and Germany had seen a genuine social revolution. They had played a full part in the life of their countries, used strikes to

Polish women employed by the Germans to work in coal mines

achieve their ends and, for the first time, had realized their economic power. A British journalist wrote: 'Women have become more alert, and more critical towards their working conditions, more inclined to rise against injustice than before the war.' The emancipation of women had begun. They won the right to vote in Great Britain in 1918, and in Germany in 1919, but in France not until 1945.

The white angels
To middle-class or high society women, the war gave opportunities for daily dedication. From the day war broke out, they rushed to become nurses. In the streets of Paris, veils and heavy capes replaced the frivolous fashions of the pre-war period.

Aristocrats adapted their private mansions in the Saint-Germain district into auxiliary hospitals; others turned their cars into ambulances. Despite the hardship, misery and horror, very few gave up their new jobs. In 1917 alone, the Red Cross enrolled 6,000 volunteers. Some of them even went to the front with motorized surgical units to assist the surgeons who operated on the battlefield, often under enemy fire.

Prisoners

With its machine-gun jammed, this German plane was defenceless and it surrendered to its French adversary, who photographed the German flyer raising his hands.

'Any soldier who surrenders or falls into enemy hands without doing everything possible to defend himself is a coward. Any soldier taken prisoner through his own carelessness or negligence, any commander who allows his men to be taken by the enemy because of lack of discipline, is guilty of a very serious offence. The Commander-in-Chief orders that anyone not wounded who is taken prisoner will, on his return, be subjected to an enquiry to ascertain whether he should be disciplined or court-martialled, especially for surrender, desertion before the enemy, or abandoning his position in the presence of the enemy. [Signed] Joffre. To all armies, 28 November 1914.'

Fortunately this order was not acted on after the armistice, and civilians never knew of it. After each offensive, captured prisoners were questioned at length by intelligence officers. Some gave no more than their name and number, others were prepared to talk about the impact of bombardment, the position of their artillery and other units, names of the commanders, the morale of the troops, and even kitchen gossip. Governments were soon confronted with the problem of feeding, guarding and managing tens and then hundreds of thousands of prisoners. Germany, whose own population was subject to rationing after 1916, had to feed, albeit badly, more than a million extra men. The men and weapons needed to keep order and prevent escapes were thus kept from the front. Some captives had only one aim, to escape and fight again. The pilot Roland Garros, who managed to escape from Germany and was finally killed in aerial combat in October 1918, was a good example. The Hague Convention, signed by all nations before the war, set out the regulations for the treatment

French prisoners, their uniforms covered with the white chalk of Champagne where the battle had taken place, are gathered in front of a cattle truck in which they will be taken to a camp in central Germany.

of prisoners, guaranteeing a minimum of decency. For example officers, including non-commissioned ones, could not be forced to work! During the war, every country tried to make profitable use of its prisoners, often with mixed results. Some found themselves breaking stones to make roads. The luckier ones lived on farms, replacing the absent men and working on the land. In this way they helped their captor's war effort. For security reasons, France sent many of its German prisoners to the North African colonies. However, most remained in camps. They organized language classes, training courses, do-it-yourself workshops, musical groups and even acting troupes. In 1914, the Red Cross in Switzerland set up information services to help families to find missing people, and get food parcels to them in the camps. They also checked on prison conditions, arranged exchanges of wounded captives, and established a minimum of relations between governments, since all embassies were closed down.

In the summer of 1918, German soldiers surrendered to the Allies in their hundreds of thousands.

War on the Screen

In 1918, Charlie Chaplin made his own film about the war. With his sense of humour the little man with the moustache ridiculed the horrors of war. The equipment of this unusual soldier included such items as a tin bath, a coffee pot. an egg-whisk, a mousetrap and a cheese grater!

Right from the start of the war, cinemas were used for propaganda purposes. In formal melodramas, the enemy were shown in exaggerated and grotesque form. With titles like *The Betrothed of 1914*, *The Traitress*, *French Women – Be on Guard!*, and *The German's Daughter*, these films always showed an innocent victim escaping German atrocities by the skin of his or her teeth.

Films made after the war by those who had seen action were very different. In *J'accuse* (1918), Abel Gance superimposed the disfigured faces of soldiers on a view of the battlefield, and men killed in action rise from the grave to tell of their sacrifice.

Not long after it had finished, the Great War became the historical setting for adventure films, such as King Vidor's *Great Parade* (1925). Screen adaptations were made of novels such as Remarque's *All Quiet on the Western Front* (Lewis Milestone, 1930), and Dorgelès's *Wooden Crosses* (Raymond Bernard, 1932). In 1937, the French film director Jean Renoir made his masterpiece, *The Grand Illusion*, which denounced war and appealed to the brotherhood of man. More recently, three films have tried to explain why it was that some men mutinied at the front and were brutally repressed by courts martial: Stanley Kubrick's *Paths of Glory* (1957), Joseph Losey's *King and Country* (1964) and Francesco Rosi's *Just Another War* (1970).

Places to Visit

If you go on holiday in northern France, there are a number of battlefields and other sites which are interesting to visit. In many countries there are also museums with war exhibits.

Sites
In Artois, north of Arras, there is the cemetery of Notre-Dame-de-Lorette and a sizeable private museum. The graves of the French killed in the battle of 1915 cover an area of 10 hectares (25 acres). A few kilometres to the east, on Vimy ridge, are the Canadian memorial, the battlefield with its trenches preserved intact, and a system of underground tunnels, part of which is open to the public. North of Reims, one can visit the 20 kilometres (12 miles) of the Chemin des Dames front. To the east, on the road to Châlons-sur-Marne, the ruins of Fort Pompelle house a museum with a big collection of German arms and helmets. Fort Vaux is the most evocative memorial of the battle of Verdun.

Museums
France
Musée de l'Armée, Hôtel des Invalides, Paris.
Verdun Memorial, Fleury-devant-Douamont, Verdun.

Belgium
Musée Royal de l'Armée et d'Histoire Militaire, Brussels.

West Germany
Bavarian Army Museum, Neues Schloss, Ingolstadt.

Italy
Italian Museum of War History, Castello Veneto, Rovereto.

Britain
National Army Museum, London.
Imperial War Museum, London.

Canada
The Canadian War Museum, 330 Sussex Drive, Ottawa, Ontario K1A OM8

Australia
Australian War Memorial, Anzac Parade, Canberra A.C.T. 2601.

A model of a French trench in 1915

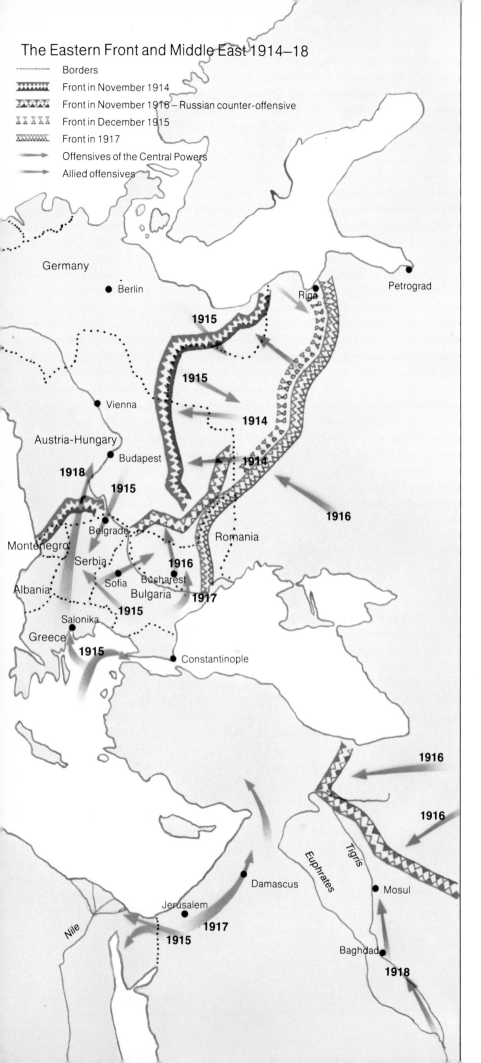

The Eastern Front and Middle East 1914–18

- ········· Borders
- ▚▚▚▚▚▚ Front in November 1914
- ▚▚▚▚▚▚ Front in November 1916 – Russian counter-offensive
- ⅄⅄⅄⅄ Front in December 1915
- ▚▚▚▚▚ Front in 1917
- ➜ Offensives of the Central Powers
- ➜ Allied offensives

Germany

● Berlin

Riga

● Petrograd

1915

1915

● Vienna

1915

Austria-Hungary

1914

● Budapest

1918

1914

1915

Montenegro

Belgrade

1916

Romania

Serbia

1916

Albania

Sofia

Bucharest

Bulgaria

1917

1915

Salonika

Greece

1915

Constantinople

1916

1916

Damascus

Euphrates

Tigris

● Mosul

Jerusalem

1917

Nile

1915

● Baghdad

1918

Important dates

1914
28 June: Franz Ferdinand assassinated
3 August: Germany declares war on France
4 August: Britain declares war on Germany
August–September: French and British retreat
30 August: Russian defeat at Tannenberg
6–11 September: Battle of the Marne
5 November: Turkey enters the war

1915
18 February: First German U-boat attack
March: start of the Dardanelles campaign
22 April: first use of poison gas
23 May: Italy enters the war
December: Serbia totally overrun

1916
February–July: German attack on Verdun
31 May: Battle of Jutland
10 June: Mecca taken by British
July–September: Battle of the Somme
August–December: Romania enters war on Allied side and is invaded

1917
1 February: total submarine war
27 February: beginnings of revolution in Russia
11 March: British take Baghdad
6 April: United States enters war
16 April: Chemin des Dames offensive
May–June: mutinies in the French army
24–25 October: Bolshevik coup and seizure of power in Russia
24 October–9 November: Italian defeat at Caporetto

1918
8 January: Wilson's Fourteen Points
March: Ludendorff offensives
3 March: peace between Germany and Russia
July: second Battle of the Marne
26 September: general Allied offensive
26–30 October: Italian victory at Vittorio Veneto
9 November: Kaiser Wilhelm II abdicates
11 November: Armistice

1919
28 June: Treaty of Versailles

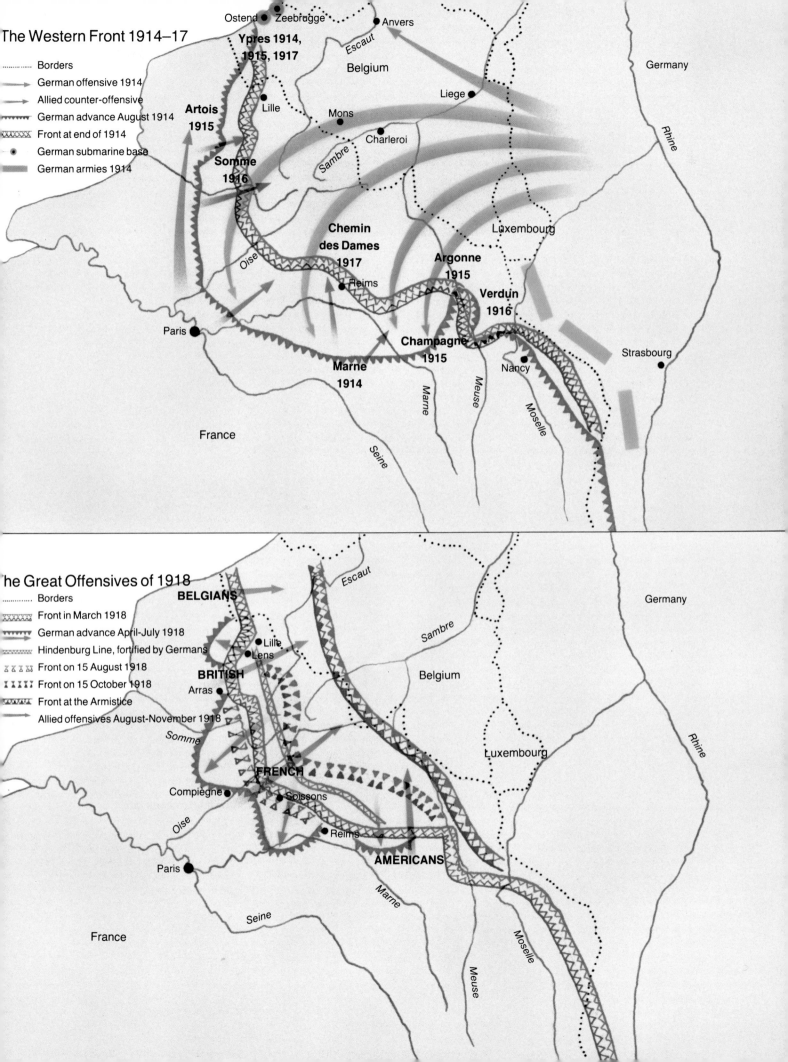

The Western Front 1914–17

- .... Borders
- → German offensive 1914
- → Allied counter-offensive
- ⋁⋁⋁ German advance August 1914
- ⧓⧓⧓ Front at end of 1914
- ⊙ German submarine base
- ▬ German armies 1914

Ostend Zeebrugge Anvers

Ypres 1914, 1915, 1917

Escaut

Belgium

Germany

Liege

Artois 1915

Lille

Mons

Charleroi

Sambre

Rhine

Somme 1916

Chemin des Dames 1917

Oise

Reims

Argonne 1915

Luxembourg

Verdun 1916

Paris

Champagne 1915

Marne 1914

Nancy

Strasbourg

Meuse

Marne

Moselle

France

Seine

The Great Offensives of 1918

- .... Borders
- ⧓⧓⧓ Front in March 1918
- ⋁⋁⋁ German advance April-July 1918
- ⧓⧓⧓ Hindenburg Line, fortified by Germans
- ⌇⌇⌇ Front on 15 August 1918
- ⌇⌇⌇ Front on 15 October 1918
- ⧓⧓⧓ Front at the Armistice
- → Allied offensives August-November 1918

BELGIANS

Escaut

Germany

BRITISH

Lille

Lens

Sambre

Belgium

Arras

Rhine

Somme

Luxembourg

FRENCH

Compiègne

Soissons

Oise

Reims

AMERICANS

Paris

Marne

Seine

Moselle

France

Meuse

Glossary

Alliance A group of countries united in a common cause
Annexation The act of adding territory to a nation
Armistice An agreement between opposing armies to halt hostilities and discuss peace terms

Central Powers Germany and Austria-Hungary, together with their allies Turkey and Bulgaria
Communism A system in which there are no social classes, and private ownership is abolished, the means of production and exchange being owned collectively by the community
Conscription Compulsory military service

Kaiser The title of a German emperor, but especially Wilhelm II

Pacifist A person who is against war and believes that peaceful means should be used to end or solve conflicts
Propaganda Information spread to improve one's own cause or undermine the cause of an enemy

Rationing A situation in which goods, such as food, are distributed in limited and controlled amounts
Reparations Compensation demanded from a defeated country by the victors of a conflict

Socialism An economic system in which means of production, distribution and exchange are collectively owned by the Community, usually through the State

Index